The Nuremberg Trial

Other books in the History Firsthand series:

The Nuremberg Trial

Mitchell Bard, *Book Editor*

Daniel Leone, *President*
Bonnie Szumski, *Publisher*
Scott Barbour, *Managing Editor*
David M. Haugen, *Series Editor*

Greenhaven Press, Inc., San Diego, California

Every effort has been made to trace the owners of copyrighted material. The articles in this volume may have been edited for content, length, and/or reading level. The titles have been changed to enhance the editorial purpose.

Library of Congress Cataloging-in-Publication Data

The Nuremberg trial / Mitchell Bard, editor.
    p. cm. — (History firsthand)
    Includes bibliographical references and index.
    ISBN 0-7377-1075-6 (pbk. : alk. paper) —
    ISBN 0-7377-1076-4 (lib. : alk. paper)
    1. War crime trials—Germany—Nuremberg. 2. Nuremberg
Trial of Major German War Criminals, Nuremberg, Germany,
1945–1946. 3. Prosecution—Germany. 4. Press and politics—
Germany. I. Bard, Mitchell, 1959– . II. Series.

KZ1176 .N87   2002
341.6'9—dc21   2001040734

Contents

Chapter 2: The Prosecution

Chapter 3: The Challenge of Being Fair

masquerading as law. He argued that many of the laws used to judge the Nazis had no legal precedent and, once established, might haunt future legal proceedings in democratic nations.

Chapter 4: The Verdicts and Conclusions

precedents that may inhibit other nations from pursuing wars of conquest and aggression.

Foreword

In his preface to a book on the events leading to the Civil War, Stephen B. Oates, the historian and biographer of Abraham Lincoln, John Brown, and other noteworthy American historical figures, explained the difficulty of writing history in the traditional third-person voice of the biographer and historian. "The trouble, I realized, was the detached third-person voice," wrote Oates. "It seemed to wring all the life out of my characters and the antebellum era." Indeed, how can a historian, even one as prominent as Oates, compete with the eloquent voices of Daniel Webster, Abraham Lincoln, Harriet Beecher Stowe, Frederick Douglass, and Robert E. Lee?

Oates's comment notwithstanding, every student of history, professional and amateur alike, can name a score of excellent accounts written in the traditional third-person voice of the historian that bring to life an event or an era and the people who lived through it. In *Battle Cry of Freedom*, James M. McPherson vividly re-creates the American Civil War. Barbara Tuchman's *The Guns of August* captures in sharp detail the tensions in Europe that led to the outbreak of World War I. Taylor Branch's *Parting the Waters* provides a detailed and dramatic account of the American Civil Rights Movement. The study of history would be impossible without such guiding texts.

Nonetheless, Oates's comment makes a compelling point. Often the most convincing tellers of history are those who lived through the event, the eyewitnesses who recorded their firsthand experiences in autobiographies, speeches, memoirs, journals, and letters. The Greenhaven Press History Firsthand series presents history through the words of first-person narrators. Each text in this series captures a significant historical era or event—the American Civil War, the

Great Depression, the Holocaust, the Roaring Twenties, the 1960s, the Vietnam War. Readers will investigate these historical eras and events by examining primary-source documents, authored by chroniclers both famous and little known. The texts in the History Firsthand series comprise the celebrated and familiar words of the presidents, generals, and famous men and women of letters who recorded their impressions for posterity, as well as the statements of the ordinary people who struggled to understand the storm of events around them—the foot soldiers who fought the great battles and their loved ones back home, the men and women who waited on the breadlines, the college students who marched in protest.

The texts in this series are particularly suited to students beginning serious historical study. By examining these firsthand documents, novice historians can begin to form their own insights and conclusions about the historical era or event under investigation. To aid the student in that process, the texts in the History Firsthand series include introductions that provide an overview of the era or event, timelines, and bibliographies that point the serious student toward key historical works for further study.

The study of history commences with an examination of words—the testimony of witnesses who lived through an era or event and left for future generations the task of making sense of their accounts. The Greenhaven Press History Firsthand series invites the beginner historian to commence the process of historical investigation by focusing on the words of those individuals who made history by living through it and recording their experiences firsthand.

Introduction: The Greatest Trial

More than half a century has elapsed since the end of World War II, and it is difficult to fully comprehend the enormity of what was by far the most destructive human endeavor in history. Battles were fought on every continent and involved more than sixty countries, affecting roughly three-quarters of the world's population. The casualty figures are staggering: More than 57 million people were killed, more than half of whom were civilians. The Soviet Union alone suffered the loss of more than 21 million people. The United States, which entered the war later than the other Allies, still had roughly three hundred thousand casualties.

Beyond these general statistics, however, were hundreds, maybe thousands, of stories of crimes committed against soldiers and civilians. These included cases of prisoners of war being murdered, sent to concentration camps, and abused; and civilians herded into ghettos and exterminated in death camps. Among the dead were 6 million Jews—two-thirds of the total living in Europe at that time—victims of Adolf Hitler's obsessive anti-Semitism. By war's end, the Allies felt justified to punish the Germans responsible for this carnage.

Establishing a Precedent

During the war the Allied nations of England, France, Russia, and the United States knew of many of the atrocities and warned the Germans that they would be held accountable after the war. The U.S. government decided not to pursue war criminals until after the Allied victory for fear of provoking reprisals against prisoners of war. Instead, officials secretly gathered evidence of war crimes for use after the war.

One argument against pursuing any case against the Germans responsible for the conduct of the war and the atrocities committed against civilians in general, and the Jews in particular, was that no international law existed to justify such a prosecution. However, this was not entirely true. Treaties had been signed foreswearing aggressive wars and a variety of conventions had been universally recognized governing the conduct of war, such as the Geneva Convention relating to the treatment of prisoners of war.

The lack of judicial precedent, however, could not be allowed to prevent the pursuit of Nazi war criminals. In law, somewhere, sometime there must be a first case that establishes the precedent. At Nuremberg, the Allies decided to prosecute Nazis for the common plan or conspiracy to wage aggressive war in violation of international law or treaties; planning, preparation for, or waging an aggressive war; violations of the international rules of war; and crimes against humanity.

The most original of the charges was the one pertaining to crimes against humanity. Nothing in the law forbids a state from murdering its own citizens, but the Allies were so horrified by the atrocities of the Germans and their collaborators that it did not seem sufficient to merely indict them for the war itself; it was also necessary to punish them specifically for the systematic murder of civilians. Moreover, the Allies needed to respond to the Germans who claimed their actions had not violated any state laws. To the Allied nations, this case would establish the laws for future crimes relating to warfare.

Justice, Not Vengeance

Many Allied officials, including England's Winston Churchill and Russia's Joseph Stalin, would have been happy to summarily execute Germans captured after the war. In the short-run, such retribution might have been satisfying and would have met with little opposition from a revenge-seeking public, but other officials, especially Justice Robert H. Jackson, the U.S. chief prosecutor at the Nuremberg Trial, believed this would be a tragic mistake. Jackson believed the Germans should be given the very type of trial they denied their opponents—one that was fair and open.

Ultimately, the four major powers—Great Britain, France, the Soviet Union, and the United States—decided to put the Germans on trial with the understanding that a fair trial implied that some or all could escape punishment if the evidence did not prove their guilt. Of course, given the amount of evidence at their disposal, the prosecutors had little doubt about the outcome.

Besides demonstrating their commitment to the rule of law, the Allies' motivation in holding a trial was to set an example for the future, to show that crimes of the magnitude committed during the war would not go unpunished. They wanted to show they could resist the temptation to exact vengeance and to hold Nazi officials and military leaders accountable for the actions of their underlings. Furthermore, they wanted to make clear to the rank-and-file that crimes could not be excused by the claim that a person was "just following orders."

One of the criticisms of the Allies was that they were pursuing a form of "victors' justice." The Nazis argued they were not doing anything different from anyone else who had waged war; they were being considered criminals only because they had failed. As the war's victors, the Allies were indeed determining all of the rules of the game whereby the losers of the war would be judged. In addition, the same standards established for determining crimes by the Germans were not applied to the Allies themselves. Though the scale cannot in any way be compared, there is no question that the Allies (especially the Soviets) were involved in incidents that could have been judged criminal. Though they had been allies during the war, by the time of the Nuremberg Trial the United States, in particular, was very uncomfortable with the Soviet Union's role in the trial because Stalin was engaging in activities in areas under his control that would undoubtedly be considered criminal by Nuremberg's standard, and yet he remained a prosecutor rather than a defendant.

A related issue was how the judges—from nations that had been victims of Nazi aggression—could objectively listen to evidence at Nuremberg. Some critics argued that the judges were necessarily biased. Defenders of the trial noted that perhaps the judges were predisposed to find the defendants guilty, but it would have been difficult to find anyone who could truly have been called neutral given the huge scope of the war.

To partially offset the sense of unfairness, the Allies allowed the defendants to choose any lawyer they wanted, including attorneys who had been Nazis. In addition, most trial rules favored the defendants or were adapted to ensure their rights were protected, such as providing German translations of all documents.

As it turned out, the fairness of the trial was borne out by the fact that not every defendant was found guilty of all the charges, a result that surprised the prosecution (though members of the team acknowledged their case had weaknesses).

The Defendants

One of the prosecution's initial difficulties was in deciding who should be tried. Many Nazis who might have been tried for war crimes fled after the war. Some were helped by the director of the German Church in Rome. Argentina proved to be one of the most popular havens for war criminals, many of whom were aided by ODESSA, an organization of SS men set up to help them. As many as ten thousand Nazis may have entered the United States. Some of them were helped by intelligence agencies interested in soliciting their help in the new cold war against communism. Operation Paper Clip was a deliberate program by the U.S. military that brought approximately sixteen hundred German scientists to America to work on various projects. For example, Arthur Rudolph became the director of the Saturn V moon rocket program. During the war he had used concentration camp laborers to work on the Nazi V-2 rocket-powered bombs.

The first priority for the Allies was to bring the people considered the leaders of the German war effort to trial. Many top officials of the Nazi Reich, however, escaped judgment. Adolf Hitler committed suicide. So did Hitler's preferred successor, Joseph Goebbels, and Heinrich Himmler, the head of the Gestapo and SS. Hitler's second in command, Martin Bormann, was ordered to flee Germany and was never captured. He was believed to have died in 1945. Adolf Eichmann, one of the principal architects of the Holocaust, escaped to Argentina. Still, a large number of Nazi ministers and generals were detained by Allied armies.

In October 1945 twenty-four people were indicted for war crimes, but not all would make it to trial in Nuremberg. For example, charges were later dropped against industrialist Gustav Krupp, who employed thousands of slave laborers in his armament factories. He did not stand trial because of his "physical and mental condition." His son, Alfried, was tried in a separate case at Nuremberg. Robert Ley, head of the German Labor Front, committed suicide after his indictment. That left twenty-two defendants, including Bormann, who could not be located and was tried in absentia.

The trial commenced at Nuremberg between October 20, 1945, and October 1, 1946. Among the defendants at Nuremberg were eight judges, one university professor, and one dentist. All of them were very well educated. In addition to the aforementioned Bormann, the other defendants were:

Karl Doenitz: Supreme commander of the navy; and in accordance with Hitler's will, the president of the Third Reich and supreme commander of the armed forces.

Hans Frank: Governor-general of occupied Poland.

Wilhelm Frick: Minister of the interior.

Hans Fritzsche: Ministerial director and head of the radio division in the propaganda ministry.

Walther Funk: President of the Reichsbank.

Hermann Göring: Reichsmarschall and chief of the air force.

Rudolf Hess: Deputy to Hitler.

Alfred Jodl: Chief of army operations.

Ernst Kaltenbrunner: Chief of the Reich Main Security Office, whose departments included the Gestapo and SS.

Wilhelm Keitel: Chief of staff of the high command of the armed forces.

Constantin von Neurath: Protector of Bohemia and Moravia.

Franz von Papen: One-time chancellor of Germany.

Erich Raeder: Grand admiral of the navy.

Joachim von Ribbentrop: Minister of foreign affairs.

Alfred Rosenberg: Minister of the occupied eastern territories.

Fritz Sauckel: Labor leader.

Hjalmar Schacht: Minister of economics.

Baldur von Schirach: Reich Youth leader.

Arthur Seyss-Inquart: Commisar of the Netherlands.

Albert Speer: Minister of armaments and war production.

Julius Streicher: Editor of the newspaper *Der Stürmer*, director of the Central Committee for the Defense Against Jewish Atrocity and Boycott Propaganda.

These twenty-one men stood as the accused. They were indicted as individuals, but it was clear that their crimes were representative of the horrors enacted by the entire Reich.

Germans Incriminate Themselves

German efficiency was the defendants' undoing in the sense that so much documentation had been produced and saved that the verdicts were considered by most observers to be a foregone conclusion. Though the Nazis made efforts at the end of the war to destroy records and blow up entire installations, such as the concentrations camps, a remarkable amount of material survived the war and was collected from all over Germany and the territories it had occupied. One of the difficult aspects of preparing for a trial was the need to collect, collate, and analyze thousands of documents in a relatively short period of time. This was also especially important because of the Nuremberg prosecutors' decision to base their case almost entirely on these documents rather than on the testimony of witnesses.

In addition to helping to establish the defendants' guilt, the documentary record was also important to ensure that a new German movement could not emerge and claim that everything said about the Nazis was just Allied propaganda. The records are even more important today as the number of actual participants in the war, and witnesses to the crimes, declines and revisionists seek to rewrite history.

Part of a Larger Conspiracy

Although modern Holocaust deniers claim the atrocities of the war did not happen or try to minimize them, the defendants did no such thing. They did not refute the evidence. Some did say they did not know what was happening or complained they were singled out for doing the same things as others who escaped arrest. Others hid behind the argument that they were only following orders and were therefore not responsible for their actions or those of their subordinates.

Though public attention naturally gravitated toward the individual defendants, they were not the only ones on trial. The prosecutors also decided to use these top officials to establish that German organizations such as the Gestapo, the military high command, and the SS were themselves criminal. The prosecutors believed, though this was one of the more heatedly debated tactics in the trial, that it would be easier to hold other individuals responsible for crimes if they were shown to be members of a criminal organization.

The prosecution also wanted to establish a precedent that would prevent the leaders from escaping justice while their underlings were punished. After all, most of the defendants could honestly claim they had never personally killed anyone. To eliminate the defense that they had not been the ones to pull the triggers, the prosecutors charged that the defendants were part of a conspiracy to commit war crimes. This was perhaps the most difficult charge to prove because it required evidence that all of the defendants knew what was going on and made decisions that directly or indirectly resulted in crimes.

A Fair Result

The press, the German people, and the general public were all able to watch the trial. The transcripts and documents were also available, so no one could accuse the Allies of misconduct. The trial was universally recognized and respected. Nevertheless, the Nuremberg Trial was an imperfect tribunal, but it was still more just by legal standards than perhaps any other created to adjudicate war crimes. The fairness of the trial was evident in the fact that three of the defendants (Schacht, von Papen, and Fritzsche) were acquitted. Still, the evidence was so overwhelming that eleven were given the death penalty, three were sentenced to life imprisonment, and four received prison terms ranging from ten to twenty years. Those who received prison sentences were sent to Spandau Prison. Those acquitted were placed in a denazification program following the trial.

After 1966 the sole inmate of Spandau Prison was Rudolf Hess, who committed suicide in 1987 at the age of ninety-two. Of the other convicted men who were given jail time, most served their full sentences. The exceptions were von Neurath, who was sentenced to fifteen years but became ill and was released in 1954 (he died in 1956); Raeder, who served less than ten years of his life sentence (and died in 1960); and Funk, who was also in failing health and was paroled in 1957 (and also died in 1960).

The defendants sentenced to death were hanged (except Göring, who committed suicide in his cell) at Spandau Prison on October 6, 1946. Their bodies were taken to Dachau and were cremated in the ovens. Their ashes were dropped into a river.

Other Trials

The expectation prior to the Nuremberg Trial was that many trials would be held and that the precedents in the Nuremberg case would be used in subsequent ones. In fact, several war crimes trials were held at Nuremberg, but when one speaks of "the Nuremberg Trial," the reference is usually to the trial of the twenty-two main defendants.

Twelve other trials were held in Nuremberg to prosecute 185 defendants for a variety of crimes. These trials included the "Medical Case" to punish the people responsible for the ghoulish experiments on concentration camp prisoners; the "I.G. Farben Case" to prosecute industrialists who sold Zyklon B, the chemical used in concentration camp gas chambers, and who constructed industrial plants at Auschwitz; and the "Einsatzgruppen Case" to try the men involved in the Nazi's mobile killing squads. The trial dealing with the mistreatment of prisoners of war was the "High Command Case." Trials were also held for the Germans responsible for individual concentration and prisoner-of-war camps. William Denson, the chief prosecutor of trials concerning the major concentration camps—Buchenwald, Flossenbürg, Mauthausen, and Dachau—tried 177 criminals in the four cases. In the Buchenwald case, for example, the evidence of atrocities was sufficient for the court to convict all thirty-one of the accused for violations of the laws and usages of war. The judges imposed twenty-two death sentences, five life terms, one ten-year term, two of fifteen years, and one of twenty years. But six death sentences were commuted to life; one to twenty years. Two life terms were reduced to twenty years, one to fifteen, and another to four years. One fifteen-year sentence was reduced to five years. One ten-year sentence was reduced to three years.

According to the UN War Crimes Commission, as of October 31, 1946, 1,108 accused war criminals were tried in Europe, 413 were sentenced to death, 485 were imprisoned, and 210 were acquitted. The United States held approximately 900 trials with 3,000 defendants. Of those tried in

Germany, 1,380 were convicted and 241 were acquitted. A total of 421 death sentences were handed down, but many were commuted. Only 136 of 194 life sentences were ultimately approved. Trials were also held at Dachau for conventional war crimes—that is, not crimes against peace or humanity. Of 1,672 tried, 426 were sentenced to death, but most were never carried out. Even among those receiving life sentences, the norm was to release the prisoners after, at most, seven years.

John J. McCloy, the U.S. high commissioner for Germany, came under tremendous pressure from the pope, the German government, and others to grant clemency to convicted war criminals. Subsequently, he commuted the sentence of Ernst von Weizsacker, a Nazi foreign office official convicted of complicity in the deaths of six thousand Jews transferred from France to Poland; commuted or reduced the sentences of all convicted concentration camp doctors; twenty of the twenty-five SS officers convicted of serving in the Einsatzgruppen; as well as Nazi industrialist Alfried Krupp. In 1951 McCloy issued a general amnesty.

Crimes in the Pacific

Although most press was focused on Nuremberg, an International Military Tribunal for the Far East was set up in Tokyo in May 1946 to try Japanese officials and military personnel who committed war crimes. A total of twenty-five men were indicted; two men died during the trial and a third was considered mentally unfit to be tried. The best-known defendant was Hideki Tojo, who had led Japan throughout the war. All of the men were found guilty, and seven, including Tojo, were sentenced to death and were hanged. Sixteen others received life sentences, and two men who had served for short periods as foreign minister received prison terms. One, Mamoru Shigemitsu, actually returned to politics and served again as Japan's foreign minister.

In 1947 the Americans shifted the remaining trials to the Philippines. The U.S. Navy also held trials on Kwajalein in the Marshall Islands for crimes committed in the Pacific.

These trials exposed more atrocities, including medical experiments conducted on Americans. Additional trials were conducted in Yokohama, Japan. The British tried criminals who had mistreated civilians and soldiers in places like Borneo, Singapore, and Burma. China, Australia, France, and Russia also held trials. Roughly fifty-six hundred Japanese were tried for war crimes in twenty-two hundred trials. More than forty-four hundred were convicted, and one thousand were executed.

The Hunt Goes On

Some people seeking justice or vengeance, such as renowned Nazi hunter Simon Wiesenthal, continue to look for Nazi war criminals. For some time there were doubts as to whether certain high officials like Martin Bormann or even Hitler had died. Those two were dead, but many others lived comfortably with different identities (and sometimes in the open) in places like Argentina, Paraguay, and Syria.

One man who was found alive was Adolf Eichmann, the SS official responsible for the deportation of Jews. Israeli secret agents tracked him down at his home on Garibaldi Street in Buenos Aires and spirited him away to Jerusalem, where he was tried and convicted. To this day, he is the only person ever to be executed in Israel.

The United States set up the Office of Special Investigation in 1979 to track down Nazis who entered the country illegally. It continues to locate these criminals and usually seeks to strip them of their American citizenship and deport them to the countries where they committed their crimes. Though the surviving Nazi war criminals are all very old and are usually in ill health, they still are being held accountable for their actions.

The Conduct of Future Wars

In recent years the world has witnessed a number of wars in which atrocities were committed that prompted calls for war crimes trials. Tribunals are now in place to judge people accused of war crimes in Rwanda and the Balkans. The precedent for holding political and military leaders accountable for their behavior during wartime is the Nuremberg Trial. On one hand, this resort to the Nuremberg precedent is a reflection of how important that trial was in establishing international law pertaining to the conduct of war. On the other hand, however, the greater objective of the people who formulated the basis for the Nuremberg Trial was to discourage future wars, and especially war crimes, by demonstrating that perpetrators would be punished. Thus, the fact that wars have continued and that horrific acts have been features of many conflicts is proof the ideal of Nuremberg has not been realized.

Chapter 1

Preparation for Trial

Chapter Preface

The war in Europe ended on May 8, 1945, when Germany surrendered. In less than six months the Allies had decided to hold war crimes trials. A dedicated staff chose defendants, established procedures, gathered and analyzed thousands of pages of documentary evidence, and renovated the building in Nuremberg in which the most prominent trial would be held. This was not an easy accomplishment, especially since many other things were going on simultaneously.

For one thing, World War II was not over. Fighting against Japan continued in the Pacific throughout the summer and ended only after the atomic bombs were dropped and the formal surrender was signed on September 2. In Europe, the Allies were involved in a variety of activities, including creating displaced-persons camps for the thousands of refugees who survived the war but could not return to their homes, rebuilding the shattered economies and infrastructure of most of the nations of Europe, and dealing with the emotional trauma of the millions of military and civilian casualties. On top of this, Allied intelligence was still seeking and arresting Nazis, who were rapidly disappearing underground or fleeing to other countries.

The pursuit of Nazi war criminals may not have been the highest postwar priority, but it was deemed sufficiently important to invest the time, money, and energy needed to quickly pull together the trial. And the Allies had never left any doubt about their determination to hold the German authorities responsible for the conduct of the war and the atrocities committed at their command. Throughout the war, the United States, in particular, said it would hold the Germans accountable and worked to gather evidence that could be used when the war was over.

The United States did not conduct the trials by itself, however; it did so in cooperation with its wartime allies. Just as during the war it was sometimes necessary for the Americans to compromise, so too were they forced to accommodate the views of the British, French, and Soviets in decisions related to the trial. The four powers had different legal traditions, different postwar objectives and international status, and had been victimized by the Nazis to different degrees.

Given the rivalries and differences, it is all the more remarkable that the Allies succeeded in creating a tribunal that would be so widely respected and make such a lasting impact on international law.

The Objectives of the Prosecution

Robert H. Jackson

In 1945, President Truman asked Supreme Court justice
Robert H. Jackson to take a leave from the bench and serve as
chief U.S. prosecutor of former German leaders during the
upcoming trial at Nuremberg. Although the basis for the trial
was decided in negotiations with the French, British, and
Soviets, Jackson was largely responsible for the legal basis of
the charter used to define the work of the International Military Tribunal. Ironically, Jackson had no experience as a prosecuting attorney, a shortcoming that was most evident during
his weak cross-examination of Hermann Göring and other
defendants. In this excerpt from the report he wrote to the
president on June 7, during the negotiations with the other
Allies regarding the trial, Jackson explains the difficulty of
his task and the weightiness of the issues. At this early junc-
ture, however, it is possible to see how Jackson formulated
most of the legal and moral principles that ultimately were
adopted in the trial.

M y dear Mr. President:
I have the honor to report accomplishments during
the month since you named me as Chief of Counsel for the
United States in prosecuting the principal Axis War Criminals. In brief, I have selected staffs from the several services,
departments and agencies concerned; worked out a plan for
preparation, briefing, and trial of the cases; allocated the

Excerpted from "Report to the President on Atrocities and War Crimes," by Robert H.
Jackson, *U.S. Department of State Bulletin*, June 7, 1945.

work among the several agencies; instructed those engaged in collecting or processing evidence; visited the European Theater to expedite the examination of captured documents, and the interrogation of witnesses and prisoners; coordinated our preparation of the main case with preparation by Judge Advocates of many cases not included in my responsibilities; and arranged cooperation and mutual assistance with the United Nations War Crimes Commission and with Counsel appointed to represent the United Kingdom in the joint prosecution.

The responsibilities you have conferred on me extend only to "the case of major criminals whose offenses have no particular geographical localization and who will be punished by joint decision of the governments of the Allies," as provided in the Moscow Declaration of November 1, 1943, by President Roosevelt, Prime Minister Churchill and Premier Stalin. It does not include localized cases of any kind. Accordingly, in visiting the European Theater, I attempted to establish standards to segregate from our case against the principal offenders, cases against many other offenders and to expedite their trial. These cases fall into three principal classes:

1. The first class comprises offenses against military personnel of the United States such, for example, as the killing of American airmen who crash-landed, and other Americans who became prisoners of war. In order to insure effective military operation, the field forces from time immemorial have dealt with such offenses on the spot. Authorization of this prompt procedure, however, had been withdrawn because of the fear of stimulating retaliation through execution of captured Americans on trumped-up charges. The surrender of Germany and liberation of our prisoners has ended that danger. The morale and safety of our own troops and effective government of the control area seemed to require prompt resumption of summary dealing with this type of case. Such proceedings are likely to disclose evidence helpful to the case against the major criminals and will not prejudice it in view of the measures I have suggested to preserve evidence and to prevent premature execution of those who

are potential defendants or witnesses in the major case. . . .

2. A second class of offenders, the prosecution of which will not interfere with the major case, consists of those who, under the Moscow Declaration, are to be sent back to the scene of their crimes for trial by local authorities. These comprise localized offenses or atrocities against persons or property, usually of civilians of countries formerly occupied by Germany. The part of the United States in these cases consists of the identification of offenders and the surrender on demand of those who are within our control. . . .

3. In a third class of cases, each country, of course, is free to prosecute treason charges in its own tribunals and under its own laws against its own traitorous nationals: Quislings, Lavals, "Lord Haw-Haws," and the like.

The consequence of these arrangements is that preparations for the prosecution of major war criminals will not impede or delay prosecution of other offenders. In these latter cases, however, the number of known offenses is likely to exceed greatly the number of prosecutions, because witnesses are rarely able satisfactorily to identify particular soldiers in uniform whose acts they have witnessed. This difficulty of adequately identifying individual perpetrators of atrocities and crimes makes it more important that we proceed against the top officials and organizations responsible for originating the criminal policies, for only by so doing can there be just retribution for many of the most brutal acts. . . .

No Freedom for Suspects

The custody and treatment of war criminals and suspects appeared to require immediate attention. I asked the War Department to deny those prisoners who are suspected war criminals the privileges which would appertain to their rank if they were merely prisoners of war; to assemble them at convenient and secure locations for interrogation by our staff; to deny them access to the press; and to hold them in the close confinement ordinarily given suspected criminals. The War Department has been subjected to some criticism from the press for these measures, for which it is fair that I should

acknowledge responsibility. The most elementary considerations for insuring a fair trial and for the success of our case
suggest the imprudence of permitting these prisoners to be
interviewed indiscriminately or to use the facilities of the
press to convey information to each other and to criminals
yet uncaptured. Our choice is between treating them as hon-
orable prisoners of war with the privileges of their ranks, or
to classify them as war criminals in which case they should
be treated as such. I have assurances from the War Department that those likely to be accused as war criminals will be
kept in close confinement and stern control. . . .

The Basis for the Trial

The time, I think, has come when it is appropriate to outline
the basic features of the plan of prosecution on which we
are tentatively proceeding in preparing the case of the
United States.

1. The American case is being prepared on the assumption that an inescapable responsibility rests upon this country to conduct an inquiry, preferably in association with others, but alone if necessary, into the culpability of those
whom there is probable cause to accuse of atrocities and
other crimes. We have many such men in our possession.
What shall we do with them? We could, of course, set them
at large without a hearing. But it has cost unmeasured thousands of American lives to beat and bind these men. To free
them without a trial would mock the dead and make cynics
of the living. On the other hand, we could execute or otherwise punish them without a hearing. But undiscriminating
executions or punishments without definite findings of guilt,
fairly arrived at, would violate pledges repeatedly given, and
would not set easily on the American conscience or be remembered by our children with pride. The only other course
is to determine the innocence or guilt of the accused after a
hearing as dispassionate as the times and the horrors we deal
with will permit, and upon a record that will leave our reasons and motives clear.

2. These hearings, however, must not be regarded in the

same light as a trial under our system, where defense is a matter of constitutional right. Fair hearings for the accused are, of course, required to make sure that we punish only the right men and for the right reasons. But the procedure of these hearings may properly bar obstructive and dilatory tactics resorted to by defendants in our ordinary criminal trials.

Nor should such a defense be recognized as the obsolete doctrine that a head of state is immune from legal liability. There is more than a suspicion that this idea is a relic of the doctrine of the divine right of kings. It is, in any event, inconsistent with the position we take toward our own officials, who are frequently brought to court at the suit of citizens who allege their rights to have been invaded. We do not accept the paradox that legal responsibility should be the least where power is the greatest. We stand on the principle of responsible government declared some three centuries ago to King James by Lord Chief Justice Coke, who proclaimed that even a King is still "under God and the law."

With the doctrine of immunity of a head of state usually is coupled another, that orders from an official superior protect one who obeys them. It will be noticed that the combination of these two doctrines means that nobody is responsible. Society as modernly organized cannot tolerate so broad an area of official irresponsibility. There is doubtless a sphere in which the defense of obedience to superior orders should prevail. If a conscripted or enlisted soldier is put on a firing squad, he should not be held responsible for the validity of the sentence he carries out. But the case may be greatly altered where one has discretion because of rank or the latitude of his orders. And of course, the defense of superior orders cannot apply in the case of voluntary participation in a criminal or conspiratorial organization, such as the Gestapo or the S.S. An accused should be allowed to show the facts about superior orders. The Tribunal can then determine whether they constitute a defense or merely extenuating circumstances, or perhaps carry no weight at all.

3. Whom will we accuse and put to their defense? We will accuse a large number of individuals and officials who were

in authority in the government, in the military establishment, including the General Staff, and in the financial, industrial, and economic life of Germany who by all civilized standards are provable to be common criminals. We also propose to establish the criminal character of several voluntary organizations which have played a cruel and controlling part in subjugating first the German people and then their neighbors. It is not, of course, suggested that a person should be judged a criminal merely because he voted for certain candidates or maintained political affiliations in the sense that we in America support political parties. The organizations which we will accuse have no resemblance to our political parties. Organizations such as the Gestapo and the S.S. were direct action units, and were recruited from volunteers accepted only because of aptitude for, and fanatical devotion to, their violent purposes.

In examining the accused organizations in the trial, it is our proposal to demonstrate their declared and covert objectives, methods of recruitment, structure, lines of responsibility, and methods of effectuating their programs. In this trial, important representative members will be allowed to defend their organizations as well as themselves. The best practicable notice will be given, that named organizations stand accused and that any member is privileged to appear and join in their defense. If in the main trial an organization is found to be criminal, the second stage will be to identify and try before regular military tribunals individual members not already personally convicted in the principal case. Findings in the main trial that an organization is criminal in nature will be conclusive in any subsequent proceedings against individual members. The individual member will thereafter be allowed to plead only personal defenses or extenuating circumstances, such as that he joined under duress, and as to those defenses he should have the burden of proof. There is nothing novel in the idea that one may lose a part of or all his defense if he fails to assert it in an appointed forum at an earlier time. In United States wartime legislation, this principle has been utilized and sustained as consistent with our concept of due process of law.

4. Our case against the major defendants is concerned with the Nazi master plan, not with individual barbarities and perversions which occurred independently of any central plan. The groundwork of our case must be factually authentic and constitute a well-documented history of what we are convinced was a grand, concerted pattern to incite and commit the aggressions and barbarities which have shocked the world. We must not forget that when the Nazi plans were boldly proclaimed they were so extravagant that the world refused to take them seriously. Unless we write the record of this movement with clarity and precision, we cannot blame the future if in days of peace it finds incredible the accusatory generalities uttered during the war. We must establish incredible events by credible evidence.

5. What specifically are the crimes with which these individuals and organizations should be charged, and what marks their conduct as criminal?

There is, of course, real danger that trials of this character will become enmeshed in voluminous particulars of wrongs committed by individual Germans throughout the course of the war, and in the multitude of doctrinal disputes which are part of a lawyer's paraphernalia. We can save ourselves from those pitfalls if our test of what legally is crime gives recognition to those things which fundamentally outraged the conscience of the American people and brought them finally to the conviction that their own liberty and civilization could not persist in the same world with the Nazi power.

Those acts which offended the conscience of our people were criminal by standards generally accepted in all civilized countries, and I believe that we may proceed to punish those responsible in full accord with both our own traditions of fairness and with standards of just conduct which have been internationally accepted. I think also that through these trials we should be able to establish that a process of retribution by law awaits those who in the future similarly attack civilization. . . .

The Crimes

Early in the Nazi regime, people of this country came to look upon the Nazi Government as not constituting a legitimate state pursuing the legitimate objective of a member of the international community. They came to view the Nazis as a band of brigands, set on subverting within Germany every vestige of a rule of law which would entitle an aggregation of people to be looked upon collectively as a member of the family of nations. Our people were outraged by the oppressions, the cruelest forms of torture, the large-scale murder, and the wholesale confiscation of property which initiated the Nazi regime within Germany. They witnessed persecution of the greatest enormity on religious, political and racial grounds, the breakdown of trade unions, and the liquidation of all religious and moral influences. This was not the legitimate activity of a state within its own boundaries, but was preparatory to the launching of an international course of aggression and was with the evil intention, openly expressed by the Nazis, of capturing the form of the German state as an instrumentality for spreading their rule to other countries. Our people felt that these were the deepest offenses against that International Law described in the Fourth Hague Convention of 1907 as including the "laws of humanity and the dictates of the public conscience."

Once these international brigands, the top leaders of the Nazi party, the S.S. and the Gestapo, had firmly established themselves within Germany by terrorism and crime, they immediately set out on a course of international pillage. They bribed, debased, and incited to treason the citizens and subjects of other nations for the purpose of establishing their fifth columns of corruption and sabotage within those nations. They ignored the commonest obligations of one state respecting the internal affairs of another. They lightly made and promptly broke international engagements as a part of their settled policy to deceive, corrupt, and overwhelm. They made, and made only to violate, pledges respecting the demilitarized Rhineland, and Czechoslovakia, and Poland, and Russia. They did not hesitate to instigate the Japanese to treacherous attack on the United States. Our people saw in this succession of events the destruction of the minimum elements of trust which can hold the community of nations together in peace and progress. Then, in consummation of their plan, the Nazis swooped down upon the nations they had deceived and ruthlessly conquered them. They flagrantly violated the obligations which states, including their own, have undertaken by convention or tradition as a part of the rules of land warfare, and of the law of the sea. They wantonly destroyed cities like Rotterdam for no military purpose. They wiped out whole populations, as at Lidice, where no military purposes were to be served. They confiscated property of the Poles and gave it to party members. They transported in labor battalions great sectors of the civilian populations of the conquered countries. They refused the ordinary protections of law to the populations which they enslaved. The feeling of outrage grew in this country, and it became more and more felt that these were crimes committed against us and against the whole society of civilized nations by a band of brigands who had seized the instrumentality of a state.

I believe that those instincts of our people were right and that they should guide us as the fundamental tests of criminality. We propose to punish acts which have been regarded as criminal since the time of Cain and have been so written in every civilized code. . . .

Is War a Crime?

Doubtless what appeals to men of good will and common sense as the crime which comprehends all lesser crimes, is the crime of making unjustifiable war. War necessarily is a calculated series of killings, of destructions of property, of oppressions. Such acts unquestionably would be criminal except that International Law throws a mantle of protection around acts which otherwise would be crimes, when committed in pursuit of legitimate warfare. In this they are distinguished from the same acts in the pursuit of piracy or brigandage which have been considered punishable wherever and by whomever the guilty are caught. But International Law as taught in the Nineteenth and the early part of the Twentieth Century generally declared that war-making was not illegal and is no crime at law. . . .

This, however, was a departure from the doctrine taught by Grotius, the father of International Law, that there is a distinction between the just and the unjust war, the war of defense and the war of aggression. . . .

By the time the Nazis came to power it was thoroughly established that launching an aggressive war or the institution of war by treachery was illegal and that the defense of legitimate warfare was no longer available to those who engaged in such an enterprise. It is high time that we act on the juridical principle that aggressive war-making is illegal and criminal.

The re-establishment of the principle of unjustifiable war is traceable in many steps. One of the most significant is the Briand-Kellogg Pact of 1928, by which Germany, Italy and Japan, in common with ourselves and practically all the nations of the world, renounced war as an instrument of national policy, bound themselves to seek the settlement of disputes only by pacific means, and condemned recourse to war for the solution of international controversies. Unless this Pact altered the legal status of wars of aggression, it has no meaning at all and comes close to being an act of deception. In 1932, Mr. Stimson, as Secretary of State, gave voice to the American concept of its effect. He said, "War between nations was renounced by the signatories of the Briand-Kellogg Treaty. This means that it has become illegal throughout practically the entire world. It is no longer to be the source and subject of rights. It is no longer to be the principle around which the duties, the conduct, and the rights of nations revolve. It is an illegal thing. . . . By that very act, we have made obsolete many legal precedents and have given the legal profession the task of reexamining many of its codes and treatises.". . .

I have left until last the first question which you and the American people are asking when can this trial start and how long will it take. I should be glad to answer if the answer were within my control. But it would be foolhardy to name dates which depend upon the action of other governments and of many agencies. Inability to fix definite dates, however, would not excuse failure to state my attitude toward the time and duration of trial.

I know that the public has a deep sense of urgency about these trials. Because I, too, feel a sense of urgency, I have proceeded with the preparations of the American case before completion of the diplomatic exchanges concerning the Tribunal to hear it and the agreement under which we are to work. We must, however, recognize the existence of serious difficulties to be overcome in preparation of the case. . . . The preparation must cover military, naval, diplomatic, political, and commercial aggressions. The evidence is scattered among various agencies and in the hands of several armies. The captured documentary evidence—literally tons of orders, records, and reports—is largely in foreign languages. Every document and the trial itself must be rendered into several languages. An immense amount of work is necessary to bring this evidence together physically, to select what is useful, to integrate it into a case, to overlook no relevant detail, and at the same time and at all costs to avoid becoming lost in a wilderness of single instances. Some sacrifice of perfection to speed can wisely be made and, of course, urgency overrides every personal convenience and comfort for all of us who are engaged in this work.

Beyond this I will not go in prophecy. The task of making this record complete and accurate, while memories are fresh, while witnesses are living, and while a tribunal is available, is too important to the future opinion of the world to be undertaken before the case can be sufficiently prepared to make a creditable presentation. Intelligent, informed, and sober opinion will not be satisfied with less.

The trial must not be protracted in duration by anything that is obstructive or dilatory, but we must see that it is fair and deliberative and not discredited in times to come by any mob spirit. Those who have regard for the good name of the

United States as a symbol of justice under law would not have me proceed otherwise.

May I add that your personal encouragement and support have been a source of strength and inspiration to every member of my staff, as well as to me, as we go forward with a task so immense that it can never be done completely or perfectly, but which we hope to do acceptably.

Respectfully yours, ROBERT H. JACKSON

International Cooperation and Concession

Robert H. Jackson

By the summer of 1945, the American public was war weary.
Most were just learning about the extent of the atrocities
committed by the Nazis. The first reports of the mass extermination of Europe's Jews, for example, were only now coming to light. Even without knowing about the concentration
camps, Americans would have wanted some measure of justice, or revenge, against the German leaders who had waged
such a ferocious war. Given the U.S. role in winning the war,
it would have been understandable if most Americans wanted
their government to handle the trials of the Nazis, but politics
and logistics required that the four major Allied powers cooperate in conducting the trial of the most prominent Nazis.
Because the United States could not act alone, U.S. chief
prosecutor Robert H. Jackson issued a statement on August
12, before the trial started, to explain the purpose of the trial
and some of the compromises necessary to accommodate the
legal traditions and political demands of America's allies.

There are some things I would like to say, particularly
to the American people, about the agreement we have
just signed.

For the first time, four of the most powerful nations have
agreed not only upon the principles of liability for war

From "Statement by Justice Jackson on War Trials Agreement," by Robert H. Jackson,
U.S. Department of State Bulletin, August 12, 1945.

crimes of persecution, but also upon the principle of individual responsibility for the crime of attacking the international peace.

Repeatedly, nations have united in abstract declarations that the launching of aggressive war is illegal. They have condemned it by treaty. But now we have the concrete application of these abstractions in a way which ought to make clear to the world that those who lead their nations into aggressive war face individual accountability for such acts.

The definitions under which we will try the Germans are general definitions. They impose liability upon war-making statesmen of all countries alike. If we can cultivate in the world the idea that aggressive war-making is the way to the prisoner's dock rather than the way to honors, we will have accomplished something toward making the peace more secure.

This, too, is the first time that four nations with such different legal systems have tried to knit their ideas of just criminal procedure into a cooperative trial. That task is far more difficult than those unfamiliar with the differences between continental and Anglo-American methods would expect. It has involved frank and critical examination by the representatives of each country of the other's methods of administering justice. Our discussions have been candid and open-minded.

The representatives of the United Kingdom have been headed by the Lord Chancellor and the Attorney General. The Soviet Republic has been represented by the Vice President of its Supreme Court and by one of the leading scholars of Soviet jurisprudence. The Provisional Government of France has sent a judge of its highest court and a professor most competent in its jurisprudence.

It would not be a happy forecast for the future harmony of the world if I could not agree with such representatives of the world's leading systems of administering justice on a common procedure for trial of war criminals.

Of course, one price of such international cooperation is mutual concession. Much to which American lawyers would be accustomed is missing in this instrument. I have not seen fit to insist that these prisoners have the benefit of all of the protections which our legal and constitutional system throws around defendants.

To the Russian and French jurist, our system seems unduly tender of defendants and to be loaded in favor of delay and in favor of the individual against the state. To us, their system seems summary and to load the procedure in favor of the state against the individual.

However, the continental system is the one the Germans themselves have employed and understand. It does not seem inappropriate that a special military commission for the trial of Europeans in Europe, for crimes committed in Europe, should follow rather largely although not entirely the European procedures. The essentials of a fair trial have been assured.

Justice Delayed

Another price of international cooperation is slow motion. No doubt Russia acting alone, or the United States, or any one country acting alone, could try these defendants in much shorter time than we can do it when we consult with each other and move along together. Our associates, for example, have a claim as good as ours to have the trial proceed in a language which they understand.

This requires a trial rendered into four languages— German, Russian, French, and English. This will be a dreary business, and there is no use trying to dodge that fact. It is a tedious prospect for me and for representatives of all the governments which will engage in it.

But I do not think the world will be poorer even if it takes a month or so, more or less, to try these men who now are prisoners and whose capacity for harm already has been overcome.

I do think the world would be infinitely poorer if we were to confess that the nations which now dominate the western world hold ideas of justice so irreconcilable that no common procedure could be devised or carried out.

No Vengeance

The danger, so far as the moral judgment of the world is concerned, which will beset these trials is that they come to be regarded as merely political trials in which the victor wreaks vengeance upon the vanquished. However unfortunate it may be, there seems no way of doing anything about the crimes against the peace and against humanity except that the victors judge the vanquished.

Experience has taught that we can hardly expect them to try each other. The scale of their attack leaves no neutrals in the world. We must summon all that we have of dispassionate judgment to the task of patiently and fairly presenting the record of these evil deeds in these trials.

We must make clear to the Germans that the wrong for which their fallen leaders are on trial is not that they lost the war, but that they started it. And we must not allow ourselves to be drawn into a trial of the causes of the war, for our position is that no grievances or policies will justify resort to aggressive war. It is utterly renounced and condemned as an instrument of policy.

I therefore want to make clear to the American people that we have taken an important step forward in this instrument in fixing individual responsibility of war-mongering, among whatever peoples, as an international crime. We have taken another in recognizing an international accountability for persecutions, exterminations, and crimes against humanity when associated with attacks on the peace of the international order.

But I want to be equally clear that to make these advances fully effective through international trials is a task of difficulty and one which will require some public patience and some understanding of the wide gulf which separates the judicial systems of the nations which are trying to cooperate in the effort.

Charter of the International Military Tribunal

Once a decision was made by the four Allied powers—Great Britain, France, the Soviet Union, and the United States—to conduct a war crimes trial, it was necessary to determine the rules by which it would be conducted. No trial of its kind had ever been held, so procedures and principles needed to be established. Some were already a part of the history of international law, but much of the trial's foundation had to be laid from scratch by the participants. Since it was decided early on that the trial would be open and every effort would be made to make it fair, it was important to make the rules clear and public. This was done in a charter for the Nuremberg Trial, which is excerpted here.

I. Constitution of the International Military Tribunal

Article 1.

In pursuance of the Agreement signed on the 8th day of August 1945 by the Government of the United States of America, the Provisional Government of the French Republic, the Government of the United Kingdom of Great Britain and Northern Ireland and the Government of the Union of Soviet Socialist Republics, there shall be established an International Military Tribunal (hereinafter called "the Tribunal") for the just and prompt trial and punishment

Excerpted from the Charter of the International Military Tribunal, London, England, August 8, 1945.

of the major war criminals of the European Axis.

Article 2.

The Tribunal shall consist of four members, each with an alternate. One member and one alternate shall be appointed by each of the Signatories. The alternates shall, so far as they are able, be present at all sessions of the Tribunal. In case of illness of any member of the Tribunal or his incapacity for some other reason to fulfill his functions, his alternate shall take his place. . . .

II. Jurisdiction and General Principles

Article 6.

The Tribunal established by the Agreement referred to in Article 1 hereof for the trial and punishment of the major war criminals of the European Axis countries shall have the power to try and punish persons who, acting in the interests of the European Axis countries, whether as individuals or as members of organizations, committed any of the following crimes.

The following acts, or any of them, are crimes coming within the jurisdiction of the Tribunal for which there shall be individual responsibility:

(a) CRIMES AGAINST PEACE: namely, planning, preparation, initiation or waging of a war of aggression, or a war in violation of international treaties, agreements or assurances, or participation in a common plan or conspiracy for the accomplishment of any of the foregoing;

(b) WAR CRIMES: namely, violations of the laws or customs of war. Such violations shall include, but not be limited to, murder, ill-treatment or deportation to slave labor or for any other purpose of civilian population of or in occupied territory, murder or ill-treatment of prisoners of war or persons on the seas, killing of hostages, plunder of public or private property, wanton destruction of cities, towns or villages, or devastation not justified by military necessity;

(c) CRIMES AGAINST HUMANITY: namely, murder, extermination, enslavement, deportation, and other inhumane acts committed against any civilian population, before or during the war; or persecutions on political, racial or religious grounds in execution of or in connection with any crime within the jurisdiction of the Tribunal, whether or not in violation of the domestic law of the country where perpetrated.

Leaders, organizers, instigators and accomplices participating in the formulation or execution of a common plan or conspiracy to commit any of the foregoing crimes are responsible for all acts performed by any persons in execution of such plan.

Article 7.

The official position of defendants, whether as Heads of State or responsible officials in Government Departments, shall not be considered as freeing them from responsibility or mitigating punishment.

Article 8.

The fact that the Defendant acted pursuant to order of his Government or of a superior shall not free him from responsibility, but may be considered in mitigation of punishment if the Tribunal determines that justice so requires.

Article 9.

At the trial of any individual member of any group or organization the Tribunal may declare (in connection with any act of which the individual may be convicted) that the group or organization of which the individual was a member was a criminal organization. . . .

Article 10.

In cases where a group or organization is declared criminal by the Tribunal, the competent national authority of any Signatory shall have the right to bring individual to trial for membership therein before national, military or occupation courts. In any such case the criminal nature of the group or organization is considered proved and shall not be questioned.

Article 11.

Any person convicted by the Tribunal may be charged before a national, military or occupation court, referred to in Article 10 of this Charter, with a crime other than of membership in a criminal group or organization and such court may, after convicting him, impose upon him punishment independent of and additional to the punishment imposed by the Tribunal for participation in the criminal activities of such group or organization.

Article 12.

The Tribunal shall have the right to take proceedings against a person charged with crimes set out in Article 6 of this Charter in his absence, if he has not been found or if the Tribunal, for any reason, finds it necessary, in the interests of justice, to conduct the hearing in his absence. . . .

III. Committee for the Investigation and Prosecution of Major War Criminals

Article 14.

Each Signatory shall appoint a Chief Prosecutor for the investigation of the charges against and the prosecution of major war criminals.

The Chief Prosecutors shall act as a committee for the following purposes:

(a) to agree upon a plan of the individual work of each of the Chief Prosecutors and his staff,

(b) to settle the final designation of major war criminals to be tried by the Tribunal,

(c) to approve the Indictment and the documents to be submitted therewith,

(d) to lodge the Indictment and the accompanying documents with the Tribunal,

(e) to draw up and recommend to the Tribunal for its approval draft rules of procedure, contemplated by Article 13 of this Charter. The Tribunal shall have the power to accept, with or without amendments, or to reject, the rules so recommended. . . .

Article 15.

The Chief Prosecutors shall individually, and acting in collaboration with one another, also undertake the following duties:

(a) investigation, collection and production before or at the Trial of all necessary evidence,

(b) the preparation of the Indictment for approval by the

Committee in accordance with paragraph (c) of Article 14 hereof,

(c) the preliminary examination of all necessary witnesses and of all Defendants,

(d) to act as prosecutor at the Trial,

(e) to appoint representatives to carry out such duties as may be assigned them,

(f) to undertake such other matters as may appear necessary to them for the purposes of the preparation for and conduct of the Trial. . . .

IV. Fair Trial for Defendants

Article 16.

In order to ensure fair trial for the Defendants, the following procedure shall be followed:

(a) The Indictment shall include full particulars specifying in detail the charges against the Defendants. A copy of the Indictment and of all the documents lodged with the Indictment, translated into a language which he understands, shall be furnished to the Defendant at reasonable time before the Trial.

(b) During any preliminary examination or trial of a Defendant he will have the right to give any explanation relevant to the charges made against him.

(c) A preliminary examination of a Defendant and his Trial shall be conducted in, or translated into, a language which the Defendant understands.

(d) A Defendant shall have the right to conduct his own defense before the Tribunal or to have the assistance of Counsel.

(e) A Defendant shall have the right through himself or through his Counsel to present evidence at the Trial in support of his defense, and to cross-examine any witness called by the Prosecution.

V. Powers of the Tribunal and Conduct of the Trial

Article 17.

The Tribunal shall have the power

(a) to summon witnesses to the Trial and to require their

attendance and testimony and to put questions to them,

(b) to interrogate any Defendant,

(c) to require the production of documents and other evidentiary material,

(d) to administer oaths to witnesses,

(e) to appoint officers for the carrying out of any task designated by the Tribunal including the power to have evidence taken on commission. . . .

Article 19.

The Tribunal shall not be bound by technical rules of evidence. It shall adopt and apply to the greatest possible extent expeditious and nontechnical procedure, and shall admit any evidence which it deems to be of probative value.

Article 20.

The Tribunal may require to be informed of the nature of any evidence before it is entered so that it may rule upon the relevance thereof.

Article 21.

The Tribunal shall not require proof of facts of common knowledge but shall take judicial notice thereof. It shall also take judicial notice of official governmental documents and reports of the United Nations, including the acts and documents of the committees set up in the various allied countries for the investigation of war crimes, and of records and findings of military or other Tribunals of any of the United Nations.

Article 22.

The permanent seat of the Tribunal shall be in Berlin. The first meetings of the members of the Tribunal and of the Chief Prosecutors shall be held at Berlin in a place to be designated by the Control Council for Germany. The first trial shall be held at Nuremberg, and any subsequent trials shall be held at such places as the Tribunal may decide. . . .

Article 24.

The proceedings at the Trial shall take the following course:

(a) The Indictment shall be read in court.

(b) The Tribunal shall ask each Defendant whether he pleads "guilty" or "not guilty."

(c) The prosecution shall make an opening statement.

(d) The Tribunal shall ask the prosecution and the defense what evidence (if any) they wish to submit to the Tribunal, and the Tribunal shall rule upon the admissibility of any such evidence.

(e) The witnesses for the Prosecution shall be examined and after that the witnesses for the Defense. Thereafter such rebutting evidence as may be held by the Tribunal to be admissible shall be called by either the Prosecution or the Defense.

(f) The Tribunal may put any question to any witness and to any defendant, at any time.

(g) The Prosecution and the Defense shall interrogate and may cross-examine any witnesses and any Defendant who gives testimony.

(h) The Defense shall address the court.

(i) The Prosecution shall address the court.

(j) Each Defendant may make a statement to the Tribunal.

(k) The Tribunal shall deliver judgment and pronounce sentence.

Article 25.

All official documents shall be produced, and all court proceedings conducted, in English, French and Russian, and in the language of the Defendant. So much of the record and of the proceedings may also be translated into the language of any country in which the Tribunal is sitting, as the Tribunal is sitting, as the Tribunal considers desirable in the interests of the justice and public opinion.

VI. Judgment and Sentence

Article 26.

The judgment of the Tribunal as to the guilt or the innocence of any Defendant shall give the reasons on which it is based, and shall be final and not subject to review.

Article 27.

The Tribunal shall have the right to impose upon a Defendant, on conviction, death or such other punishment as shall be determined by it to be just.

Article 28.

In addition to any punishment imposed by it, the Tribunal shall have the right to deprive the convicted person of any stolen property and order its delivery to the Control Council for Germany.

Article 29.

In case of guilt, sentences shall be carried out in accordance with the orders of the Control Council for Germany, which may at any time reduce or otherwise alter the sentences, but may not increase the severity thereof. If the Control Council for Germany, after any Defendant has been convicted and sentenced, discovers fresh evidence which, in its opinion, would found a fresh charge against him, the Council shall report accordingly to the Committee established under Article 14 hereof, for such action as they may consider proper, having regard to the interests of justice.

The Work of Building a Case

Seymour Peyser

Though the defendants at Nuremberg were presumed to be guilty, the prosecutors went to great lengths to collect evidence to leave no doubt in the minds of either the judges or the public as to their crimes. This process was a massive undertaking that ultimately unearthed thousands of documents. Though the litigators are always the more glamorous attorneys in a trial, it is often the lawyers working behind the scenes to prepare the case that determine the outcome. Seymour Peyser was one of the lawyers responsible for preparing documents at Nuremberg. Among his jobs were to collect affidavits from the German police, judiciary, and press declaring the impact of Nazism on their lives and establishing the German chain of command to help prove who was responsible for actions taken during the war. In this excerpt from an interview conducted by Bruce M. Stave and Michele Palmer, Peyser explains his job and what it was like to participate in the trial.

In 1933 Hitler comes to power. Were there no discussions at Harvard College and Columbia Law School?

It was the kind of discussion one would have about a distant country. Yes, I remember this clown that I had read about in the paper, [who] had suddenly become something to be serious about. Yes, he had this frightful anti-Semitism [which] was such an important part of his whole program and his whole being. Sure, Hitler was something that everyone learned to hate. He was the devil. But there was no intellectual awareness of the size of this and I have looked back on it many, many times. It didn't really ring true to me until Nuremberg, until I got actually involved in reading and preparing for presentation. The size of it was something that shocked me and millions of others.

There were a few articles in the American papers—not much—and there were other articles in other magazines that I would occasionally get to look at. My parents were not politically conscious. I guess they would have been regarded as middle of the road and probably as Jews living in New York would have been regarded as Democrats. I knew that there were concentration camps and that this was a recurrence of the pogroms that had existed in Germany, Poland, and Russia and the kind of things that my grandparents had fled from, and that it was getting out of hand and getting to be enormous.

What transpired that brought you to Nuremberg?

Lots of things. How did I end up on Justice [Robert H.] Jackson's legal staff? Number one, in my first three and a half years in the army, I had started as a seventh-grade private and by the time Nuremberg started I was a major in the Judge Advocate General's department. . . .

I also had been editor of the *Columbia Law Review* and a good many of my predecessors and contemporaries on the *Law Review* had already in a few years distinguished themselves and they had applied and been selected. So the people that I think whose influence got me accepted were the late Harold Leventhal who had been the editor-in-chief of *Columbia Law Review* a year before my year (and before he died was a most highly respected judge in the Circuit Court of Appeals for the District of Columbia) and Ben Kaplan. Ben was one of the closest friends of Telford Taylor. It was chiefly on the recommendations of people like Harold Leventhal, Ben Kaplan, and a lawyer long gone, Warren Farr, with whom I had served in the army for a few months. . . .

It was in early August [1945] that we flew to Nuremberg

and the trial started on the 20th of November. I was gone by Christmas, back home.

Personal Preparation

What preparation did you have to go over and what was it like when you first got there?

Preparation to go over, there was really none. I didn't speak German. I can bluff a little bit in a number of languages, but I knew that we had on the staff all kinds of translators and interpreters. I did some fast reading about the Nazis in a matter of weeks before I got onto a plane. . . . Somehow we got to London.

We lived in a drafty old place in Mayfair. The office was equally drafty. It was June, I remember. I remember shivering in June in London. I remember what we used to call Willow Run, which was the Grosvenor House main ballroom, served 3,000 meals to American army officers every day, stationed in and around London.

It was a strange time because the war in Europe was over and there was a kind of sighing of relief. It was a time of difficulties and shortages. Nobody had seen an orange in years. Here I was in the company of people I looked up to. I shook hands once in London with Justice Jackson. I only talked with him a couple of times in Nuremberg. He was quite aloof from the staff, but it was an opportunity for me to renew my acquaintance with Ben Kaplan, who was older and Harold Leventhal, whom I knew well, and two or three others on the staff whom I had known, either in law school or at the JAG school or one way or the other, like Warren Farr.

We were planning our presentation, not knowing really very much about it. The only thing I could read in those days was the charter that had been agreed upon originally at the Potsdam Conference among Truman, Stalin, and Churchill. As Telford Taylor in his book explains, there had been various plans. It was a monumental job to take the legal systems of four different countries, particularly with the Russian and French system being so far from the Anglo-American, and creating a system to try the major Nazi criminals. It wasn't clear in the beginning what they were going to be tried for, until the charter was fully written and approved. There were all kinds of problems, some of which had an impact on me, problems like who was going to represent and defend these 22 major Nazi defendants. That became an issue that wasn't decided until mid-October of 1945.

In London, what I did was to read as much as I could of the work papers that had been prepared, many of them by the British, along with Telford Taylor, who had been one of the early leaders in working out the procedures. In many ways the fact that these four countries could work together was an achievement of great moment [in 1945], and that they could agree on a method of approaching the thing.

What most people still to this day forget is that these were military trials. This was a military tribunal and as far as the United States was concerned, it was convened by the president of the United States in his capacity as commander in chief, and the same is true of his majesty, King George VI. I don't even venture to know the origin of the authority in France or the Soviet Union.

I read as much as I could. Then I would get as much as I could of the translated writings of the Hitler group, so-called intellectuals of the Nazi movement way back to the *putsch* in Munich in the 1920s. And I read some of the so-called intellectual documents that had nothing to do with politics. This was the Aryan superiority. These were works of people like [Alfred] Rosenberg, like Robert Ley. Then I found myself in a plane on the way to Nuremberg. . . .

In Among the German People

Did you have much interaction with the ordinary German public?

Very little in any kind of organized fashion. I remember we started out two different ways. I don't remember how, but I did visit a couple of families who lived in Nuremberg and I got a picture of what life was like. It was bleak. These were upper-middle-class people, I would guess. They spent most of the time in my presence justifying their existence and explaining how they were really not Nazis. This got to be a standard refrain whenever you would talk with a German. . . .

Nuremberg itself physically was something that had great effect on me. I don't know how much you have seen of the pictures of what Nuremberg looked like in 1945. It had been the target of a bombing attack on two nights [by] American and British bombers. The old city, which I had visited in 1930, [a] beautiful medieval city, was in ruins, just a mass of rubble, and people were living in that rubble. It was unsanitary, I'm sure, but these were Germans. These were not long-time homeless people. They were Germans and very proud of their ability to cope, and they had managed to create a little city in the ruins of the old buildings.

I didn't meet many Germans and I had some serious doubts as to whether I would want to. I don't know how many Jews were still around. I would think there were practically none still living in Nuremberg at the time.

It seemed to me to be appropriate [as a site for the trials] for a variety of reasons. For one thing, the big stadium was there, which had been the site for many of these enormous rallies that Hitler had. It had been the place for the so-called Nuremberg Laws, the [anti-Jewish] edicts that came out in Nuremberg at that time.

It was a small city and from that point of view was difficult. It was not as big as Munich or Berlin or Frankfurt. It was literally a small town compared to them, and there weren't hotel facilities for all the visitors we had. Of course, nobody sat down to figure out this thing as a tourist attraction, but suddenly the tribunal found itself the center of all the media. God knows what would have happened in 1995, but in 1945 we had enough reporters to fill a whole castle, and that's where they lived, Walter Cronkite, Andy Logan who still writes for *The New Yorker,* a few others still around. The Faber Castle was where the press was located. The total staff was estimated to be almost a thousand, including 75 American lawyers.

Incidentally, [it was] as capable and as skilled a group of young lawyers as you could imagine at any time. For people like Donovan and Alderman and Jackson, what they had already accomplished made their reputations. In the case of the others, consider what they were going to accomplish. Among 75 lawyers you had deans of law schools, many professors, many judges, presidents of the American Bar Association. [It was] quite a group. I had a gag that I used on another occasion: Of all these eminent people, I was the only one I never heard of. [laughs]

German Organization

Was there a particular incident or an individual that stands out?

Yes, I'd say there were a couple of incidents in my few months in Nuremberg that stand out. . . .

One was in either late September or early October—I think it was September 1945. I worked directly under Ben Kaplan. My assignment was to deal not with the aggressive war path, but to paint the whole picture of the Nazi state and the Nazi party during the whole period before the war, beginning in the early 1930s until the time of the war, and gather in manageable form some evidence about what Hitler and what the Nazis had done to the judiciary, to the bar, to the press, to the police, to medicine, etc.

I remember sitting at a very early stage with Ben Kaplan in his office at the Palace of Justice and suddenly realizing that here we were as lawyers before a tribunal of judges who couldn't be assumed to know all of the things which we knew. It's the old problem of judicial notice that trial lawyers deal with regularly. We still had to prove what was the structure of the Nazi state and the Nazi party. How do you do that? To whom does box A respond, and when you get to that box A-1, where do you go from there?

The first job was, in effect, to draw a chart, find out what the whole organization was. We were helped immeasurably by the German mentality because they have always been so methodical and so precise about these things. They had the need to know, I guess, who each of them was responsible to. I had the assignment, given to me by Ben Kaplan, to draw

Mounds of Evidence

Though the idea of bringing Germans to trial after the war originated long before the war ended, little work was done to prepare for such an event. Consequently, after the war, the Allies had to rush to collect evidence for the trial at Nuremberg. Fortunately, the Germans were scrupulous about documenting their activities and had failed to destroy most of their records before they fell into Allied hands. Though the Allies certainly would have had a more complete record if they had had more time to prepare, they still assembled an astounding amount of material that was effectively used to prosecute the Germans and their collaborators at Nuremberg and in many other trials. One member of the prosecution team gives a summary of the material at their disposal.

Thirty-three persons testified for the prosecution. Sixty-one defense witnesses, in addition to nineteen of the defendants, testified for the defense. The prosecution introduced into evidence a number of affidavits taken from witnesses, subject, however, to the witnesses' being called to testify in court if the defense demanded. The testimony of 143 witnesses was given for the defense in the form of written answers to interrogatories.

The Tribunal appointed commissioners to hear evidence relating to the organizations named as criminal in the indictment. The commissioners heard 101 witnesses for the defense and received 1,809 affidavits signed by other witnesses. Thirty-eight thousand affidavits, signed by 155,000 people, were filed for the Leadership Corps of the Party, 136,215 for the SS, 10,000 for the SA, 7,000 for the SD, 3,000 for the General Staff and High Command, and 2,000 for the Gestapo.

This tremendous volume of evidence constitutes the record of the Hitler regime in Germany as received by the International Military Tribunal.

Foreword by Robert G. Storey in Whitney Harris, *Tyranny on Trial*. Dallas: Southern Methodist University Press, 1954.

a chart or to find a chart that we could present to the tribunal showing how the whole thing looked.

We learned right away that everything was in twos. There were the state and the party, and they were separate organizations, both, of course, led by Hitler. In the party he was the führer, in the state he was the chancellor. But he and his henchmen maintained this dual existence all along the line. So we looked it up and found, yes, the Germans did have charts of the state and the party. Trouble was that they were losing the war by 1943, 1944, and 1945 and they didn't bring their charts up to date. So how were we going to do that? How were we going to have it authenticated?

Someone came up with the proposition that Robert Ley, who was the head of the Labor Front, also had the title of vice president in charge of vice presidents—in charge of organization. Who better than he?

So we got him out of prison and following the required rules of the game at that time, I was in the Documentation Division, not in the Interrogation Division. Somehow or other the legal staff was divided between litigators and documentary organizers. I was in documentation. So we got Ley and arranged a meeting in a room next to the prison, and this is a day that stands out in my memory. It was in late September of 1945. I wasn't allowed to ask the questions, even though it was my job to prepare the chart. I had to bring along a lieutenant colonel from the Interrogation Division and I told him what questions to ask. He asked them and we sat next to each other. . . .

The Labor Leader

We traipsed into this room. Ley was 55 years old at the time. He had a bad cold, wore an off-white sweater that was unraveling at the elbow, and as we each came by, he clicked his heels and bowed. He immediately understood the insignia on my shoulder and he clicked his heels and bowed and said, "Herr Major." I had spent the night before reading some of the stuff he had written about the blood of the Jews running in the streets, incredible things, and I hated the son of a bitch. I remember that I had organized my intense feeling against him and he looked much older than 55 because he was ill.

So we sat down and started and we showed him the 1942 or 1943 charts. It was a series of the same questions. "Is that correct?" pointing to a box. Translated into German. *"Ya, das is richtig."* Yes, that is correct. This went on. *"Nein, das ist nicht richtig."* He said, "Well, because in 1944 we changed that and we put that department under this department."

We spent a good three hours with him because [there were] two big charts. The charts ended up on the wall of the courtroom. They were bigger than this whole wall and we ended up by being able to say that these had been authenticated by the top specialist in the Nazi hierarchy.

After we were with him two hours (everybody smoked in those days so he was getting a little bit flaky in his answers and you could see that his mind was really not all there), I handed him a cigarette, which he took immediately and lit, grateful for it. That cleared his mind so he could answer the next series of questions.

I realized suddenly that this was a human being. This guy was breathing badly because he had a bad cold. He wasn't a good specimen, but he was human and I no longer had that intensity of feeling that I had when I entered the room. I hadn't been trained for that kind of intensive long-time, stick-to-it hatred, and I have never forgotten that. . . .

Just to finish the story of Robert Ley—that night he killed himself. He hanged himself on a GI towel in the bathroom and the then-colonel in charge of the prison was transferred to a beat in Staten Island.

How did you feel when you heard that he committed suicide?

I wasn't sad. My immediate thought was, "Is that in any way going to affect the work we put into this?" I didn't have that kind of a feeling of concern for him; it's just that I wasn't good at this business of intense and continuous hating, which underlay the entire war for so many of us. I had a strong disgust for Ley, but here was somebody who was alive and then suddenly was not. In a human way I sympathized with this despicable man and said, "Well, he's better off." The remainder of his life was certainly not going to be a pleasant one and he would undoubtedly have been one of those with the most severe punishment. He would have been executed along with a number of them.

But that was one story. The other, you asked generally for human stories. I guess that is one of the reasons for this process. The other was an interesting one. It had to do with the lawyers for the defendant. This being a military tribunal, if you took the standard operating procedure in American and I suppose British military law, the court-martial is convened by the commanding general, whoever that may be. In the case of the Nuremberg Trials it was Commander-in-Chief Harry S. Truman. The prosecutor, known as the trial judge advocate, is appointed by that commanding general. Generally speaking, in military tribunals the defense counsel is also appointed, and under the Articles of War of the United States (and I assume similar rules in Britain), the defendant has the privilege of requesting civilian counsel, if civilian counsel is immediately available. It's a matter of convenience, again the decision [is] to be made by the commanding general, who is in this case the one who creates the trial.

Nazi Lawyers

The Americans and the British wanted to use the method used in our military tribunals because they were concerned that lawyers for these 22 characters, 22 defendants, would themselves be Nazis and we would be giving people prominence, simply as a professional matter, that they were not entitled to, and that it should be something that should be decided on a case-by-case method. There should be defense counsel and if the defendant makes a case for why he wants a civilian lawyer and a civilian lawyer is in other respects satisfactory, okay.

So the Americans and British went to a meeting in Berlin in October—early October, [or] late September. I was not there, obviously. This would only be, I think, the very top level of the organization; not only the chief of counsel, but representatives of the judges met with them on that occasion. The French and the Russians were violently opposed to this. They wanted the Germans to have their own lawyers because from the French point of view and to some extent I guess the Russians', they wanted to avoid the possibility that if the defendants exercised their choice or indicated their choice, they would invariably pick an American or a Briton and never a Frenchman or a Russian. So it ended two to two and that meant that the Americans and the British didn't feel that strongly about it.

It was decided that the defendants would retain their own counsel. They had, in many cases, the preeminent lawyers who were still alive. I remember the lawyer for [Hermann] Göring and for [Dr. Hjalmer] Schacht [was a] distinguished, elderly gentleman. All counsel wore the normal robes of a German lawyer, except for the lawyer for Admiral Dönitz, who was the assistant chief judge advocate of the German navy, who wore the uniform of the German navy into the courtroom until October 1946—one of the things that the Americans and British wanted to avoid. In any event, that's what happened.

What interested me was that we knew, sitting in Nuremberg, that this was a subject of dispute and had not been fully decided. It occurred to me that I might be facing a problem. One of the first things I had done when I reached Nuremberg, before I got onto this business of the structure of the state and other interesting jobs which I had, [was] to go over the list of all the roles that Hermann Göring had had and prepare a definitive list of them and have him sign off that these were the jobs that he did, which I did. He had some 25 or 30 different roles during the Nazi period, during that 15-year period. Therefore, I was a little bit more up on Göring than some others of us, [although] certainly not as much as those who had studied this as a life work.

Here I am late one evening in the bar at the Grand Hotel considering what would happen if Göring said, "That's him. I want that lawyer. I want an American Jew representing me." It might have been an offbeat kind of thing, but it was conceivable. He was clearly the brightest of the defendants, nobody ever doubted that. He didn't doubt it and none of the other 20 who were there doubted it. . . .

Anyway, what would have happened? It wouldn't have been possible for me to say, "Well, I'm sorry but I won't do it." I'm in the army. This could be an order. As it happened, I thought about it considerably because in Manila at about the same time or a little after, an old friend of mine, Frank Riel, had been ordered by General [Douglas] MacArthur to defend [Japanese General Tomoyuki] Yamashita and he had not wanted to. He had been told by his senior commanders, "What you want to do is not relevant here. Do it." And he did. . . .

At any rate, it was a purely theoretical thing and never did happen, but many times I thought to write something along those lines, a fictitious treatment.

Again, by lucky accident, I was general counsel of United Artists Corporation in the 1950s and in that capacity served as a kind of technical advisor to Stanley Kramer on *Judgment at Nuremberg*. . . .

Is it fair to say that the Americans were running the trial?

No, it's not fair. They were certainly the dominant people. I would say the Americans were the host country and they were the dominant operating group, but the British worked very much with the Americans, and the British had some very competent and very hard-working lawyers. The French lawyers were bookish, professor types who never seemed to be getting out into the real world. The Russians seemed impatient and wanted to get on with the hanging. Everything that they did thereafter made that clear. . . .

No Innocents

Was there in general a presumption of guilt?

Yes, sure there was. A presumption in feeling, but you got American and British lawyers who are trained to think otherwise. The fact that three of the defendants were acquitted is an indication that that meant something. The Russians certainly didn't vote for acquitting [Hans] Fritzsche. He was the head of the radio section of the press under [Paul Joseph] Goebbels. You know why he was one of the 21 charged with being principal criminals? Because he was one of the few people that the Russians had captured. He was captured in their zone and they had him physically and everybody else had been dug up by the victorious people from the other countries.

How could the four powers stand in judgment when the Russians were already starting their takeover of the Balkan States and the French had violated the Geneva Convention by mistreating prisoners?

It was more than just that. We knew of particular incidents where the Russians particularly had been involved. Yes, there was a sense of unease, but not very much we could do about it except go through with it. We couldn't stop in the middle and say, "Well, one of our victorious countries is also guilty. Would they please stand in the dock?" Yes, we knew about it. . . .

What's your feeling about Nuremberg justice?

My feeling, very frankly, was that I was persuaded there was enough of a background to justify a trial and that it was much better to go through this process. Certainly there was enough evidence under the classic war crimes definitions, the rules of land warfare, as it's called. Nobody could object to the evidence that American prisoners and American hospital workers and medics, had been dealt with in violation of the old conventions going back to the beginning of the twentieth century.

The important thing is that they added two other basic counts. One was the planning and waging of an aggressive war. This bothered a lot of people who felt they were being more realistic saying that the victors in any war are going to claim that the vanquished were trying to wage an aggressive war. The Serbs are now doing the same thing, so I can understand that argument.

The final one, which is what I think has interested the people of the world and the media, is the crimes against humanity. There's no precedent for people being tried for this. . . .

Public Perceptions

When you returned to America, did you have the sense that people in the U.S. understood what was happening in Nuremberg?

No, because many thinking people were asking similar questions about *ex post facto* justice. I don't think that many of them knew about the Katyn massacre [in Russia in the spring 1940] that the Russians were guilty of. I don't think that was common knowledge, or that the French had been guilty of violations of the traditional war crimes conventions.

This was a pretty big show. It was not so much the importance of it as, you know, you've got this incredible guy, Göring. To be sure there would be nothing comparable if it had been on television. . . . But you had Göring, with his jowls hanging down. He had lost 100 pounds, was very bright, listening and taking advantage of every question, every translation. He understood English very well and therefore had a great advantage.

I was told by people who were there and whom I respected that Göring toyed with Jackson. Jackson made the mistake of asking questions when he did know what the answer was going to be. You had him and you had this mask-like face of Rudolf Hess sitting right next to him, and you had a bunch of small, evil men like [Alfred] Rosenberg and [Julius] Streicher and [Fritz] Sauckel, all of whom were really directly involved in genocide.

You also had the generals and the admirals, an entirely different cast of characters. You wondered how they allowed themselves to get into this thing and by the same token, you realized that they never had been trained to avoid it. They just did what came naturally to them. This is quite a cast, in many ways much more exciting as a theatrical attraction than *Judgment at Nuremberg*. Even more exciting than Spencer Tracy. . . .

Was Nuremberg the greatest trial in history?

I don't think it was the greatest trial in history, but I think it was one of the great theatrical events of the judiciary in that area.

I think with all of its limitations, and it certainly had many, and all of the errors that were made there, I think the world is better off that these four countries did what they did, rather than shooting all the defendants.

Any human venture can be said to be futile in an absolute way. Of course the judges are people with feet of clay. Of course the judging countries are defective, as ours will always be. It's not by itself the greatest trial in history. It's not by itself going to prevent other aggressive wars or other unspeakable genocides, but it's something that can be used to mobilize people and persuade people.

Chapter 2

The Prosecution

HISTORY
FIRSTHAND

Chapter Preface

Many books have been written about the Nuremberg Trial, but to understand the scope of the nearly year-long case it is necessary to examine the actual trial records. They were published almost immediately after the trial—in twenty-two volumes of documents and testimony.

The prosecution's case at Nuremberg was not as simple and clear-cut as it might appear. The prosecutors could not simply point to the twenty-two Nazis in the courtroom and show that they had murdered millions of innocent people. In fact, none was accused of personally killing anyone. The charges were actually broader, aimed at demonstrating that they were part of an organized campaign to wage aggressive war and engage in genocide.

In addition to probing the individual responsibility of the defendants, the trial covered the criminality of groups and organizations, persecution of the church, economic looting, and the persecution of the Jews. Any one of these aspects of the war could have merited a trial of its own.

The individual defendants were also chosen carefully to represent a wide range of responsibilities and duties within the German Reich. For example, Alfred Jodl, Hermann Göring, and Karl Doenitz were top military commanders who waged the war. Wilhelm Frick, Albert Speer, and Hjalmar Schacht were government ministers who used the bureaucratic machinery of the state to build Hitler's war machine. Alfred Rosenberg and Hans Frank governed territories conquered by the Germans and were on the frontline of the campaign to exterminate the Jews. Julius Streicher and Hans Fritzsche were responsible for propaganda that helped incite people and indoctrinate them with hatred. Ernst Kaltenbrunner directed the dreaded Gestapo and SS.

The fact that these defendants only ordered killings but

did not "pull the trigger" made the prosecution more challenging, but the prevailing judgment that this defense was unsound would ultimately prevent high-level officials from escaping responsibility. The prosecution was not interested, at least at the initial stage, in punishing the average soldier or party official; the goal was to bring to justice the men and women who gave and followed the orders to commit atrocities worthy of being called war crimes.

The Prosecution's Opening Statement

Robert H. Jackson

> The opening statement in a criminal trial is usually designed
> to give an overview of the prosecution's case, explain the rea-
> son for the prosecution, highlight the evidence, and fore-
> shadow the links that will be made between the crimes and
> the defendants. Chief counsel Robert H. Jackson had an awe-
> some responsibility in his opening statement because the eyes
> of the world were on Nuremberg waiting to see if the Nazis
> would be punished for their actions and if they could be tried
> with any measure of impartiality. Jackson clearly understood
> his role and adroitly explained the importance of the case in
> the context of world affairs; however, he also made the point
> that this prosecution had some similarities to more common
> trials in which individuals seek to evade responsibility either
> by claiming that they were simply following orders or that
> they had no direct involvement in the crime. In the following
> excerpts from his speech, Jackson gives an excellent
> overview of the charges and the evidence, confronts many of
> the objections to the trial and challenges to its legal underpin-
> nings, and, perhaps most important, argues forcefully that no
> one should be above the law. Jackson was a legal scholar who
> was appointed to the Supreme Court by President Roosevelt
> in 1941. He took a leave of absence to serve as chief prosecu-
> tor at the Nuremberg Trial.

Excerpted from Robert H. Jackson's opening statement to the International Military Tribunal at Nuremberg, November 21, 1945.

The wrongs which we seek to condemn and punish have been so calculated, so malignant, and so devastating, that civilization cannot tolerate their being ignored, because it cannot survive their being repeated. That four great nations, flushed with victory and stung with injury stay the hand of vengeance and voluntarily submit their captive enemies to the judgment of the law is one of the most significant tributes that Power has ever paid to Reason.

This Tribunal, while it is novel and experimental, is not the product of abstract speculations nor is it created to vindicate legalistic theories. This inquest represents the practical effort of four of the most mighty of nations, with the support of 17 more, to utilize international law to meet the greatest menace of our times—aggressive war. The common sense of mankind demands that law shall not stop with the punishment of petty crimes by little people. It must also reach men who possess themselves of great power and make deliberate and concerted use of it to set in motion evils which leave no home in the world untouched. It is a cause of that magnitude that the United Nations will lay before Your Honors. . . .

Unfortunately the nature of these crimes is such that both prosecution and judgment must be by victor nations over vanquished foes. The worldwide scope of the aggressions carried out by these men has left but few real neutrals. Either the victors must judge the vanquished or we must leave the defeated to judge themselves. After the first World War, we learned the futility of the latter course. The former high station of these defendants, the notoriety of their acts, and the adaptability of their conduct to provoke retaliation make it hard to distinguish between the demand for a just and measured retribution, and the unthinking cry for vengeance which arises from the anguish of war. It is our task, so far as humanly possible, to draw the line between the two. We must never forget that the record on which we judge these defendants today is the record on which history will judge us tomorrow. . . .

If these men are the first war leaders of a defeated nation

to be prosecuted in the name of the law, they are also the first to be given a chance to plead for their lives in the name of the law. Realistically, the Charter of this Tribunal, which gives them a hearing, is also the source of their only hope. It may be that these men of troubled conscience, whose only wish is that the world forget them, do not regard a trial as a favor. But they do have a fair opportunity to defend themselves—a favor which these men, when in power, rarely extended to their fellow countrymen. Despite the fact that public opinion already condemns their acts, we agree that here they must be given a presumption of innocence and we accept the burden of proving criminal acts and the responsibility of these defendants for their commission. . . .

The Nazi conspiracy, as we shall show, always contemplated not merely overcoming current opposition but exterminating elements which could not be reconciled with its philosophy of the state. It not only sought to establish the Nazi "new order" but to secure its sway, as Hitler predicted, "for a thousand years." Nazis were never in doubt or disagreement as to what these dissident elements were. They were concisely described by Colonel General Von Fritsch, on 12/11/1938, in these words:

> Shortly after the first war I came to the conclusion that we would have to be victorious in three battles if Germany were to become powerful again: 1. The battle against the working class—Hitler has won this. 2. Against the Catholic Church, perhaps better expressed against Ultramontanism. 3. Against the Jews.

The Battle Against the Working Class

. . . When Hitler came to power, there were in Germany three groups of trade unions. The General German Trade Union Confederation (ADGB) with 28 affiliated unions, and the General Independent Employees Confederation (AFA) with 13 federated unions together numbered more than 4.5 million members. The Christian Trade Union had over 1.25 million members.

The working people of Germany, like the working people

of other nations, had little to gain personally by war. . . .

The first Nazi attack was upon the two larger unions. On 4/21/1933 an order not even in the name of the Government, but of the Nazi Party was issued by the conspirator Robert Ley as "Chief of Staff of the political organization of the NSDAP," applicable to the Trade Union Confederation and the Independent Employees Confederation. It directed seizure of their property and arrest of their principal leaders. . . .

All funds of the labor unions, including pension and benefit funds, were seized [on 5/2/1933]. Union leaders were sent to concentration camps. A few days later, on 5/10/1933, Hitler appointed Ley leader of the German Labor Front (Deutsche Arbeitsfront) which succeeded to the confiscated union funds. . . . On 6/24/1933 the remaining Christian Trade Unions were seized, pursuant to an order of the Nazi Party signed by Ley.

On 5/19/1933, this time by a government decree, it was provided that "trustees" of labor appointed by Hitler, should regulate the conditions of all labor contracts, replacing the former process of collective bargaining. On 11/30/1934 a decree "regulating national labor" introduced the Fuehrer Principle into industrial relations. It provided that the owners of enterprises should be the "Fuehrer" and the workers should be the followers. The "enterprise-Fuehrer" should "make decisions for employees and laborers in all matters concerning the enterprise." It was by such bait that the great German industrialists were induced to support the Nazi cause, to their own ultimate ruin.

Not only did the Nazis dominate and regiment German labor but they forced the youth into the ranks of the laboring people thus led into chains. Under a compulsory labor service decree on 6/26/1935 young men and women between the ages of 18–25 were conscripted for labor. . . . The productive manpower of the German nation was in Nazi control. By these steps the defendants won the battle to liquidate labor unions as potential opposition and were enabled to impose upon the working class the burdens of preparing for aggressive warfare. . . .

The Battle Against the Churches

The Nazi Party always was predominantly anti-Christian in its ideology. But we who believe in freedom of conscience and of religion base no charge of criminality on anybody's ideology. It is not because the Nazi themselves were irreligious or pagan, but because they persecuted others of the Christian faith that they become guilty of crime, and it is because the persecution was a step in the preparation for aggressive warfare that the offense becomes one of international consequence. To remove every moderating influence among the German people and to put its population on a total war footing, the conspirators devised and carried out a systematic and relentless repression of all Christian sects and churches.

We will ask you to convict the Nazis on their own evidence. [Hitler's secretary] Martin Bormann, in 6/1941, issued a secret decree on the relation of Christianity and National Socialism. The decree provided:

> For the first time in German history the Fuehrer consciously and completely has the leadership of the people in his own hand. With the Party, its components, and attached units the Fuehrer has created for himself and thereby the German Reich leadership an instrument which makes him independent of the church. All influences which might impair or damage the leadership of the people exercised by the Fuehrer with help of the NSDAP, must be eliminated. More and more the people must be separated from the churches and their organs, the pastors. Of course, the churches must and will, seen from their viewpoint, defend themselves against this loss of power. But never again must an influence on leadership of the people be yielded to the churches. This (influence) must be broken completely and finally.

> Only the Reich Government and by its direction the Party, its components, and attached units have a right to leadership of the people. Just as the deleterious influences of astrologers, seers, and other fakers are eliminated and suppressed by the State, so must the possibility of church influence also be totally removed. Not until this has happened, does the State leadership have influence on the individual citizens. Not until then are people and Reich secure in their existence for all the future.

Crimes Against the Jews

. . . The most savage and numerous crimes planned and committed by the Nazis were those against the Jews. Those in Germany in 1933 numbered about 500,000. In the aggregate, they had made for themselves positions which excited envy, and had accumulated properties which excited the avarice of the Nazis. They were few enough to be helpless and numerous enough to be held up as a menace.

Let there be no misunderstanding about the charge of persecuting Jews. What we charge against these defendants is not those arrogances and pretensions which frequently accompany the intermingling of different peoples and which are likely, despite the honest efforts of government, to produce regrettable crimes and convulsions. It is my purpose to show a plan and design, to which all Nazis were fanatically committed, to annihilate all Jewish people. These crimes were organized and promoted by the Party leadership, executed and protected by the Nazi officials, as we shall convince you by written orders of the Secret State Police itself.

The persecution of the Jews was a continuous and deliberate policy. It was a policy directed against other nations as well as against the Jews themselves. Anti-Semitism was promoted to divide and embitter the democratic peoples and to soften their resistance to the Nazi aggression. . . .

The persecution policy against the Jews commenced with nonviolent measures such as disfranchisement and discriminations against their religion, and the placing of impediments in the way of success in economic life. It moved rapidly to organized mass violence against them, physical isolation in ghettos, deportation, labor, mass starvation, and extermination. The Government, the party formations indicted before you as criminal organizations, the Secret State Police, the Army, private and semi-public associations, and "spontaneous" mobs that were carefully inspired from official sources, were all agencies that were concerned in this persecution. Nor was it directed against individual Jews for personal bad citizenship or unpopularity. The avowed purpose was the destruction of the Jewish people as a whole, as an end in itself, as a measure of preparation for war, and as a discipline of conquered peoples.

The conspiracy or common plan to exterminate the Jew was so methodically and thoroughly pursued, that despite the German defeat and Nazi prostration this Nazi aim largely has succeeded. Only remnants of the European Jewish population remain in Germany, in the countries which Germany occupied, and in those which were her satellites or collaborators. Of the 9.6 million Jews who lived in Nazi-dominated Europe, 60% are authoritatively estimated to have perished. 5.7 million Jews are missing from the countries in which they formerly lived, and over 4.5 million cannot be accounted for by the normal death rate nor by immigration; nor are they included among displaced persons. History does not record a crime ever perpetrated against so many victims or one ever carried out with such calculated cruelty. . . .

The most serious of the actions against Jews were outside of any law, but the law itself was employed to some extent. There were the infamous Nuremberg decrees of 9/15/1935. The Jews were segregated into ghettos and put into forced labor; they were expelled from their professions; their property was expropriated; all cultural life, the press, the theater and schools were prohibited them. . . .

As the German frontiers were expanded by war, so the campaign against the Jews expanded. The Nazi plan never was limited to extermination in Germany; always it contemplated extinguishing the Jew in Europe and often in the world. In the West, the Jews were killed and their property taken over. But the campaign achieved its zenith of savagery in the East. The eastern Jew has suffered as no people ever suffered. . . .

If I should recite these horrors in words of my own, you would think me intemperate and unreliable. Fortunately, we need not take the word of any witness but the Germans themselves. I invite you now to look at a few of the vast number of captured German orders and reports that will be offered in evidence, to see what a Nazi invasion meant. We will present such evidence as the report of Einsatzgruppe

(Action Group) A of 10/15/1941 which boasts that in over-running the Baltic States, "Native anti-Semitic forces were induced to start pogroms against the Jews during the first hours after occupation. . . ." The report continues:

From the beginning it was to be expected that the Jewish problem in the East could not be solved by pogroms alone.

In accordance with the basic orders received, however, the cleansing activities of the Security Police had to aim at a complete annihilation of the Jews. Special detachments reinforced by selected units—in Lithuania partisan detachments, in Latvia units of the Latvian auxiliary police—therefore performed extensive executions both in the towns and in rural areas. The actions of the execution detachments were performed smoothly.

The sum total of the Jews liquidated in Lithuania amounts to 71105. During the pogroms in Kovno 3800 Jews were eliminated, in the smaller towns about 1200 Jews. In Latvia, up to now a total of 30000 Jews were executed. Five hundred were eliminated by pogroms in Riga.

. . . There are reports which merely tabulate the numbers slaughtered. An example is an account of the work of Einsatzgruppen of SIPO and SD in the East, which relates that:

In Estonia all Jews were arrested immediately upon their arrival at Wehrmacht. Jewish men and women above the age of 16 and capable of work were drafted for forced labor. Jews were subjected to all sorts of restrictions and all Jewish property was confiscated. All Jewish males above the age of 16 were executed, with the exception of doctors and elders. Only 500 of an original 4,500 Jews remained. Thirty-seven thousand, one hundred eighty persons have been liquidated by the SIPO and SD in White Ruthenia during October. In one town, 337 Jewish women were executed for demonstrating a 'provocative attitude.' In another, 380 Jews were shot for spreading vicious propaganda.

And so the report continues, listing town after town, where hundreds of Jews were murdered. . . .

Other accounts tell not of the slaughter so much as of the

depths of degradation to which the tormentors stooped. For example, we will show the report made to Defendant [Alfred] Rosenberg about the army and the SS in the area under Rosenberg's jurisdiction, which recited the following:

> Details: In presence of SS man, a Jewish dentist has to break all gold teeth and fillings out of mouth of German and Russian Jews before they are executed.

> Men, women and children are locked into barns and burned alive.

> Peasants, women and children are shot on the pretext that they are suspected of belonging to bands.

. . . I shall not dwell on this subject longer than to quote one more sickening document which evidences the planned and systematic character of the Jewish persecutions. I hold a report written with Teutonic devotion to detail, illustrated with photographs to authenticate its almost incredible text, and beautifully bound in leather with the loving care bestowed on a proud work. It is the original report of the SS Brigadier General Stroop in charge of the destruction of the Warsaw Ghetto, and its title page carries the inscription "The Jewish ghetto in Warsaw no longer exists." It is characteristic that one of the captions explains that the photograph concerned shows the driving out of Jewish "bandits"; those whom the photograph shows being driven out are almost entirely women and little children. It contains a day-by-day account of the killings mainly carried out by the SS organization, too long to relate, but let me quote General Stroop's summary:

> The resistance put up by the Jews and bandits could only be suppressed by energetic actions of our troops day and night. The Reichsfuehrer SS ordered, therefore, on 4/23/1943, the cleaning out of the ghetto with utter ruthlessness and merciless tenacity. I, therefore, decided to destroy and burn down the entire ghetto without regard to the armament factories. These factories were systematically dismantled and then burned. Jews usually left their hideouts, but frequently remained in the burning buildings and

jumped out of the windows only when the heat became unbearable. They then tried to crawl with broken bones across the street into buildings which were not afire. Sometimes they changed their hideouts during the night into the ruins of burned buildings. Life in the sewers was not pleasant after the first week. Many times we could hear loud voices in the sewers. SS men or policemen climbed bravely through the manholes to capture these Jews. Sometimes they stumbled over Jewish corpses: sometimes they were shot at. Tear gas bombs were thrown into the manholes and the Jews driven out of the sewers and captured. Countless numbers of Jews were liquidated in sewers and bunkers through blasting. The longer the resistance continued the tougher became the members of the Waffen SS, Police and Wehrmacht who always discharged their duties in an exemplary manner. Frequently Jews who tried to replenish their food supplies during the night or to communicate with neighboring groups were exterminated.

"This action eliminated," says the SS commander, "a proved total of 56,065. To that, we have to add the number killed through blasting, fire, etc., which cannot be counted."

We charge that all atrocities against Jews were the manifestation and culmination of the Nazi plan to which every defendant here was a party. I know very well that some of these men did take steps to spare some particular Jew for some personal reason from the horrors that awaited the unrescued Jew. Some protested that particular atrocities were excessive, and discredited the general policy. While a few defendants may show efforts to make specific exceptions to the policy of Jewish extermination, I have found no instance in which any defendant opposed the policy itself or sought to revoke or even modify it. . . .

Toward an Aggressive War

The purpose as we have seen, of getting rid of the influence of free labor, the churches, and the Jews was to clear their obstruction the precipitation of aggressive war. If aggressive warfare in violation of treaty obligation is a matter of international cognizance the preparations for it must also be of concern to the international. Terrorism was the chief instrument for securing the cohesion of the German people in war purposes.

Moreover, the cruelties in Germany served as atrocity practice to discipline the membership of the criminal organization to follow the pattern later in occupied countries. . . .

War of Aggression

I will not prolong this address by detailing the steps leading to the war of aggression which began with the invasion of Poland on 9/1/1939. The further story will be unfolded to you from documents including those of the German High Command itself. . . .

Not the least incriminating are the minutes of Hitler's meeting with his high advisers. As early as 11/5/1937 Hitler told Defendants Goering, Raeder, and Neurath, among others, that German rearmament was practically accomplished and that he had decided to secure by force, starting with a lightning attack [on] Czechoslovakia and Austria, greater living space for German Europe no later than 1943–1945 and perhaps as early as 1938. . . .

On 8/22/1939 Hitler again addressed members of the High Command, telling them when the start of military operations would be ordered. He disclosed that for propaganda purposes, he would provocate a good reason. "It will make no difference," he announced, "whether this reason will sound convincing or not. After all, the victor will not be asked whether he talked the truth or not. We have to proceed brutally. The stronger is always right." On 11/23/1939, after the Germans had invaded Poland, Hitler made this explanation:

> For the first time in history we have to fight on only one front, the other front is at present free. But no one can know how long that will remain so. I have doubted for a long time whether I should strike in the East and then in the West. Basically I did not organize the armed forces in order not to strike. The decision to strike was always in me. Earlier or later I wanted to solve the problem. Under pressure it was decided that the East was to be attacked first.

We know the bloody sequel. Frontier incidents were staged. Demands were made for cession of territory. When

Poland refused, the German forces invaded on 9/1/1939. Warsaw was destroyed; Poland fell. The Nazis, in accordance with plan, moved swiftly to extend their aggression throughout Europe and to gain the advantage of surprise over their unprepared neighbors. Despite repeated and solemn assurances of peaceful intentions, they invaded Denmark and Norway on 4/9/1940; Belgium, The Netherlands and Luxembourg on 5/10/1940; Yugoslavia and Greece on 4/6/1941.

As part of the Nazi preparation for aggression against Poland and her allies, Germany, on 8/23/1939, had entered into a non-aggression pact with Soviet Russia. It was only a delaying treaty intended to be kept no longer than necessary to prepare for its violation. On 6/22/1941, pursuant to long-matured plans, the Nazis hurled troops into Soviet territory without any declaration of war. The entire European world was aflame.

Conspiracy with Japan

The Nazi plans of aggression called for use of Asiatic allies and they found among the Japanese men of kindred mind and purpose. . . .

On 9/27/1940 the Nazis concluded a German-Italian-Japanese 10-year military and economic alliance by which those powers agreed "to stand by and cooperate with one another in regard to their efforts in Greater East Asia and regions of Europe respectively wherein it is their prime purpose to establish and maintain a new order of things."

On 3/5/1941 a top-secret directive was issued by Defendant [Wilhelm] Keitel. It stated that the Fuehrer had ordered instigation of Japan's active participation in the war and directed that Japan's military power has to be strengthened by the disclosure of German war experiences and support of a military, economic, and technical nature has to be given. The aim was stated to be to crush England quickly thereby keeping the United States out of the war. . . .

The proofs in this case will also show that the leaders of Germany were planning war against the United States from its Atlantic as well as instigating it from its Pacific approaches. A captured memorandum from the Fuehrer's headquarters, dated 10/29/1940, asks certain information as to air bases and supply and reports further that: "The Fuehrer is at present occupied with the question of the occupation of the Atlantic islands with a view to the prosecution of war against America at a later date. Deliberations on this subject are being embarked upon here.". . .

Crimes in the Conduct of War

Even the most warlike of peoples have recognized in the name of humanity some limitations on the savagery of warfare. Rules to that end have been embodied in international conventions to which Germany became a party. This code had prescribed certain restraints as to the treatment of belligerents. The enemy was entitled to surrender and to receive quarter and good treatment as a prisoner of war. We will show by German documents that these rights were denied, that prisoners of war were given brutal treatment and often murdered. . . .

It was ordered that captured English and American airmen should no longer be granted the status of prisoners of war. They were to be treated as criminals and the Army was ordered to refrain from protecting them against lynching by the populace. The Nazi Government, through its police and propaganda agencies, took pains to incite the civilian population to attack and kill airmen who crash-landed. . . .

Similarly, we will show Hitler's top secret order, dated 10/18/1942, that commandos, regardless of condition, were "to be slaughtered to the last man" after capture. We will [show] how the circulation of secret orders, one of which was signed by [Rudolph] Hess, to be passed orally to civilians, that enemy fliers or parachutists were to be arrested or liquidated. By such means were murders incited and directed. . . .

Civilized usage and conventions to which Germany was a party had prescribed certain immunities for civilian populations unfortunate enough to dwell in lands overrun by hostile armies. The German occupation forces, controlled or commanded by men on trial before you, committed a long series of outrages against the inhabitants of occupied territory that would be incredible except for captured orders and captured reports which show the fidelity with which those orders were executed. . . .

The Nazi purpose was to leave Germany's neighbors so weakened that even if she should eventually lose the war, she would still be the most powerful nation in Europe. Against this background, we must view the plan for ruthless warfare, which means a plan for the commission of War Crimes and Crimes against Humanity.

Hostages in large numbers were demanded and killed. Mass punishments were inflicted, so savage that whole communities were extinguished. . . .

Slave Labor and Looting

Perhaps the deportation to slave labor was the most horrible and extensive slaving operation in history. On few other subjects is our evidence so abundant or so damaging. In a speech made on 1/25/1944 the Defendant [Hans] Frank, Governor General of Poland, boasted, "I have sent 1.3 million Polish workers into the Reich." The Defendant [Fritz] Sauckel reported that "out of the 5 million foreign workers who arrived in Germany not even 200000 came voluntarily.". . .

Not only was there a purpose to debilitate and demoralize the economy of Germany's neighbors for the purpose of destroying their competitive position, but there was looting and pilfering on an unprecedented scale. We need not be hypocritical about this business of looting. I recognize that no army moves through occupied territory without some pilfering as it goes. Usually the amount of pilfering increases as discipline wanes. If the evidence in this case showed no looting except of that sort, I certainly would ask no conviction of these defendants for it.

But we will show you that looting was not due to the lack of discipline or to the ordinary weaknesses of human nature. The German organized plundering, planned it, disciplined it, and made it official just as he organized everything else, and then he compiled the most meticulous records to show

that he had done the best job of looting that was possible under the circumstances. And we have those records.

The Defendant Rosenberg was put in charge of a systematic plundering of the art objects of Europe by direct order
of Hitler dated 1/29/1940. On 4/16/1943 Rosenberg reported
that up to the 7th of April, 92 railway cars with 2775 cases
containing art objects had been sent to Germany; and that
53 pieces of art had been shipped to Hitler direct, and 594
to the Defendant [Hermann] Goering. The report mentioned
something like 20000 pieces of seized art and the main locations where they were stored.

Moreover this looting was glorified by Rosenberg. Here
we have 39 leather-bound tabulated volumes of his inven-
tory, which in due time we will offer in evidence. One cannot but admire the artistry of this Rosenberg report. The
Nazi taste was cosmopolitan. Of the 9455 articles inventoried, there were included 5255 paintings, 297 sculptures,
1372 pieces of antique furniture, 307 textiles, and 2224
small objects of art. Rosenberg observed that there were approximately 10000 more objects still to be inventoried.
Rosenberg himself estimated that the values involved would
come close to a billion dollars. . . .

The Law

Of course, it was, under the law of all civilized peoples, a
crime one man with his bare knuckles to assault another.
How did it come that multiplying this crime by a million,
and adding fire arms to bare knuckles, made it a legally innocent act? The doctrine was that one could not be regarded
as criminal for committing the usual violent acts in the conduct of legitimate warfare. The age of imperialistic expan-
sion during the eighteenth and nineteenth centuries added
the foul doctrine, contrary to the teachings of early Christian and international law scholars such as [seventeenth century Dutch scholar Hugo] Grotius, that all wars are to be regarded as legitimate wars. The sum of these two doctrines
was to give war-making a complete immunity from accountability to law.

This was intolerable for an age that called itself civilized. Plain people with their earthy common sense, revolted at such fictions and legalisms so contrary to ethical principles and demanded checks on war immunities. Statesmen and international lawyers at first cautiously responded by adopting rules of warfare designed to make the conduct of war more civilized. The effort was to set legal limits to the violence that could be done to civilian populations and to combatants as well.

The common sense of men after the first World War demanded, however, that the law's condemnation of war reach deeper, and that the law condemn not merely uncivilized ways of waging war, but also the waging in any way of uncivilized wars—wars of aggression. The world's statesmen again went only as far as they were forced to go. Their efforts were timid and cautious and often less explicit than we might have hoped. But the 1920's did outlaw aggressive war.

The re-establishment of the principle that there are unjust wars and that unjust wars are illegal is traceable in many steps. One of the most significant is the Briand-Kellogg Pact of 1928, by which Germany, Italy, and Japan, in common with practically all nations of the world, renounced war as an instrument of national policy, bound themselves to seek the settlement of disputes only by pacific means, and condemned recourse to war for the solution of international controversies. . . .

Any resort to war—to any kind of a war—is a resort to means that are inherently criminal. War inevitably is a course of killings, assaults, deprivations of liberty, and destruction of property. An honestly defensive war is, of course, legal and saves those lawfully conducting it from criminality. But inherently criminal acts cannot be defended by showing that those who committed them were engaged in a war, when war itself is illegal. The very minimum legal consequence of the treaties making aggressive wars illegal is to strip those who incite or wage them of every defense the law ever gave, and to leave war-makers subject to judgment by the usually accepted principles of the law of crimes.

But if it be thought that the Charter, whose declarations concededly bind us all, does contain new law I still do not shrink from demanding its strict application by this Tribunal. The rule of law in the world, flouted by the lawlessness incited by these defendants, had to be restored at the cost to my country of over a million casualties, not to mention those of other nations. I cannot subscribe to the perverted reasoning that society may advance and strengthen the rule of law by the expenditure of morally innocent lives but that progress in the law may never be made at the price of morally guilty lives. . . .

The Crime Against Peace

A basic provision of the Charter is that to plan, prepare, initiate, or wage a war of aggression, or a war in violation of international treaties, agreements, and assurances, or to conspire or participate in a common plan to do so, is a crime.

It is perhaps a weakness in this Charter that it fails itself define a war of aggression. . . .

I suggest that an "aggressor" is generally held to be that state which is the first to commit any of the following actions:

(1) Declaration of war upon another state;

(2) Invasion by its armed forces, with or without a declaration of war, of the territory of another state;

(3) Attack by its land, naval, or air forces, with or without a declaration of war, on the territory, vessels or aircraft of another state; and

(4) Provision of support to armed bands formed in the territory of another state, or refusal, notwithstanding the request of the invaded state, to take in its own territory, all the measures in its power to deprive those bands of all assistance or protection.

And I further suggest that it is the general view that no political, military, economic, or other considerations shall serve as an excuse or justification for such actions; but exercise of the right of legitimate self-defense, that is to say, resistance to an act of aggression, or action to assist a state which has been subjected to aggression, shall not constitute a war of aggression.

It is upon such an understanding of the law that our evidence of a conspiracy to provoke and wage an aggressive war is prepared and presented. By this test each of the series of wars begun by these Nazi leaders was unambiguously aggressive. . . .

Our position is that whatever grievances a nation may have, however objectionable it finds the status quo, aggressive warfare is illegal means for settling those grievances or for altering those conditions. It may be that the Germany of the 1920's and 1930's faced desperate problems, problems that would have warranted the boldest measures short of war. All other methods—persuasion, propaganda, economic competition, diplomacy—were open to an aggrieved country, but aggressive warfare was outlawed. These defendants did make aggressive war, a war in violation of treaties. They did attack and invade their neighbors in order to effectuate a foreign policy which they knew could not be accomplished by measures short of war. And that is as far as we accuse or propose to inquire. . . .

Individual Responsibility

The Charter recognizes that one who has committed criminal acts may not take refuge in superior orders nor in the doctrine that his crimes were acts of states. These twin principles working together have heretofore resulted in immunity for practically everyone concerned in the really great crimes against peace and mankind. Those in lower ranks were protected against liability by the orders of their superiors. The superiors were protected because their orders were called acts of state. Under the Charter, no defense based on either of these doctrines can be entertained. Modern civilization puts unlimited weapons of destruction in the hands of men. It cannot tolerate so vast an area of legal irresponsibility. . . . Of course, we do not argue that the circumstances under which one commits an act should be disregarded in judging its legal effect. A conscripted private on a firing squad cannot expect to hold an inquest on the validity of the execution. The Charter implies common sense limits to liability just as it places common sense limits upon immunity. But none of these men before you acted in minor parts. Each of them was entrusted with broad discretion and exercised great power. Their responsibility is correspondingly great and may not be shifted to that fictional being, "the State", which cannot be produced for trial, cannot testify, and cannot be sentenced.

The Charter also recognizes a vicarious liability, which responsibility recognized by most modern systems of law, for acts committed by others in carrying out a common plan or conspiracy to which a defendant has become a party. I need not discuss the familiar principles of such liability. Every day in the courts of countries associated in this prosecution, men are convicted for acts that they did not personally commit, but for which they were held responsible because of membership in illegal combinations or plans or conspiracies. . . .

Making Nations Answerable to the Law

I am too well aware of the weaknesses of juridical action alone to contend that in itself your decision under this Charter can prevent future wars. Judicial action always comes after the event. Wars are started only on the theory and in the confidence that they can be won. Personal punishment, to be suffered only in the event the war is lost, will probably not be a sufficient deterrent to prevent a war where the warmakers feel the chances of defeat to be negligible.

But the ultimate step in avoiding periodic wars, which are inevitable in a system of international lawlessness, is to make statesmen responsible to law. And let me make clear that while this law is first applied against German aggressors, the law includes, and if it is to serve a useful purpose it must condemn aggression by any other nations, including those which sit here now in judgment. We are able to do away with domestic tyranny and violence and aggression by those in power against the rights of their own people only when we make all men answerable to the law. This trial represents mankind's desperate effort to apply the discipline of the law to statesmen who have used their powers of state to attack the foundations of the world's peace and to commit aggressions against the rights of their neighbors. . . .

Civilization asks whether law is so laggard as to be utterly helpless to deal with crimes of this magnitude by criminals of this order of importance. It does not expect that you can make war impossible. It does expect that your juridical action will put the forces of international law, its precepts, its prohibitions and, most of all, its sanctions, on the side of peace, so that men and women of good will, in all countries, may have "leave to live by no man's leave, underneath the law."

Indicting Organizations as Criminals

Telford Taylor

Most of the attention of the Nuremberg Trial was directed at the individual defendants, and for good reason: They were sitting in the dock, were individually responsible for many of the worst atrocities of the war and were, in most instances, interesting characters. The trial, however, was not just about those individuals. The prosecutors also decided to try the German organizations responsible for the conduct of the war and the associated crimes. These included the military high command that made most military decisions, the dreaded Gestapo and the notorious SS. The belief was that it would be impossible to have individual trials for all of the war criminals, but the responsible parties could still be held responsible if they were members of an organization declared to be criminal. The legal and philosophical basis for these charges was shaky and provoked much debate among the Allies, and the difficulty of proving the indictment is evident in this excerpt by Telford Taylor, one of the American prosecutors involved in presenting a portion of this part of the case. Taylor's account comes from his memoir of Nuremberg, published forty-six years after the trials.

O n July 30, 1946, when the Tribunal commenced receiving evidence dealing with the German organiza-

Excerpted from *The Anatomy of the Nuremberg Trials*, by Telford Taylor. Copyright © 1992 by Telford Taylor. Used by permission of Alfred A. Knopf, a division of Random House, Inc.

tions indicted under Article 9 of the Charter, it was only six weeks short of two years since Colonel Murray Bernays had first proposed such a procedure. It was about one year since Bernays had resigned from the American prosecution staff.

Bernays's motivation had been his (generally shared) belief that in the SS and other large Nazi organizations, there were hundreds of thousands of war criminals—so many that individual trials were impossible—who could only be punished on the basis of their proven membership in an organization declared criminal as an entity. . . .

In December and January, my colleagues and I had presented evidence against the several organizations named in the Indictment. . . . The Tribunal then called upon prosecution and defense counsel to state their views, and, from February 28 to March 2, 1946, the Tribunal heard arguments, which were helpful, but far from conclusive on the issues.

In accordance with Article 9 of the Charter, in October 1945 the Tribunal had ordered that notices of the impending trials of the organizations should be sent throughout occupied Germany. Notices were sent to the press, to the internment and prisoner-of-war camps where many of the organization members were to be found, and to others, through suitable channels. A mass of letters, affidavits, and applications to be heard in support of the organizations was received. The SS members alone sent 136,000 affidavits, confronting the Tribunal's Secretariat with staggering problems of interpretation and examination. . . .

Attacking the "Organization" of the Nazi Party

In November 1945, on the third day of the trial, Ralph Albrecht had given the Tribunal a short lecture on the organizational structure of the Nazi Party, with emphasis on its Leadership Corps, from Hitler at the top down to the lowly *Block* and *Zellen* officials who had no real authority and were generally unpaid, part-time, nonuniformed helpers. Not much more was heard about these matters until December 17, when Colonel Storey began presenting the prosecution's evidence against the indicted organizations, beginning with the Leadership Corps.

The Indictment described the Corps as "a distinctive and elite group within the Nazi Party" and "the central core of the common plan or conspiracy" described in Count One. The concluding paragraph of the Indictment provided:

> The prosecution expressly reserves the right to request . . . that Political Leaders of subordinate grades or ranks or of other types or classes, to be specified by the Prosecution, be excepted from further proceedings in this Case, but without prejudice to other proceedings or actions against them.

Plainly the purpose of the last provision came from awareness that charging *all* Nazi members with criminality would be both ridiculous and unmanageable. But while there was no denying that the *whole* Nazi Party was an "organization," could the same be said if the lower branches of the organizational tree were severed? Was a part of the Party an "organization"? . . .

Storey had argued that the Leadership Corps was the "directing arm" of the Party and therefore could be treated as a "group" or "organization," but he carried the problem no further. When Jackson argued before the Tribunal on February 28, 1946, he adopted the position that the Leadership Corps included all Nazi Party officials from the Fuehrer down to the *Zellenleiter,* "but not members of the staff" of the three lowest categories. However sensible, this action highlighted the assumed power of the prosecution to select and vary the indicted portions of the Nazi Party.

Storey's evidence was by no means devoid of documentary material implicating some members of the Nazi Party in crimes against Jews, mistreatment of enemy airmen forced to land in Germany, and other wartime offenses against the Geneva Conventions. But the amount of solidly proven crimes committed by Party officials was small indeed compared to the testimony and documentation implicating the denizens of [Heinrich] Himmler's evil empire [the SS and the Gestapo], and this relative paucity of Party crimes raised questions of the extent of the members' knowledge of crimes committed in their own ranks. And when [defense counsel Dr.] Servatius called his witnesses, it soon became clear that he was shooting at this target in particular.

Going from the high to the low ranks, Servatius called a *Gauleiter* from Hamburg, a *Kreisleiter* from Oldenburg, an *Ortsgruppenleiter* from the Allgäu, and a *Blockleiter* from Nuremberg. Of course all of them minimized the pernicious aspects of the Party's actions and their ignorance of concentration camps and the massacre of Jews. As for international affairs, they had wanted the Anschluss with Austria and recovery of the former German colonies, but had not expected to go to war for these aims.

The prosecution was able to make a few dents in this bland presentation. . . .

But overall the cross-examination of Servatius's witnesses was not profitable. . . .

The Defense Raises Objections

Servatius began his final argument, presented on August 22, in accordance with the Tribunal's procedure, after all the defense counsel for the indicted organizations had called their witnesses and offered their documents. It was a forceful analysis of the legal basis of the prosecution's case against his organizational clients. He pointed out, quite rightly, that many of the prosecution's accusations—establishment of a dictatorship, dissolution of the trade unions, Kristallnacht and other anti-Jewish laws, and antichurch actions—were not war crimes and not within the Tribunal's jurisdiction unless they could be tied into preparation for aggressive war, which was unlikely. He questioned the "group" or "organization" status of the slice of the Nazi Party selected by the prosecution. And he criticized, as had all his colleagues, the juridical validity of inflicting criminal penalties on individual members without giving them all the rights of defendants.

As for the crimes attributed by the prosecution to the Party leaders, Servatius contended that there was no evidence to connect them with initiating aggressive war, that they had no responsibility for the concentration camps or the atrocities committed under Himmler's auspices, that there was no proof that lynching captured enemy aviators was "tolerated and approved of by the Political Leaders," that service in the Party was only nominally voluntary, and that much of the prosecution's evidence concerned matters, such as anti-Semitic and antichurch activities, which were not crimes within the reach of the Charter.

In these contentions, Servatius was not seeking to prove that war crimes had not been committed by Political Leaders, but to question the prosecution's assumption that most of the Political Leaders, numbering some 600,000 members, were aware of or implicated in the Party's crimes. . . .

Turning to Military and Paramilitary "Organizations"

The Tribunal next turned to what might well be called the "Himmler Organization of Groups," comprising both civil and military groups. According to the Indictment, the charges were brought against the Schutzstaffel (Protection Squad) of the Nazi Party, which Himmler had commanded since 1929 and which included the Waffen (armed) SS, which fought with and under the command of the army, but remained administratively under Himmler, and "all other offices and departments" of the SS, including the RSHA (Reich Security Main Office), originally led by [Reinhard] Heydrich and after his death by [Dr. Ernst] Kaltenbrunner. This included among its numerous departments the Sicherheitsdienst (SD, Security Service), the Sicherheitspolizei (SIPO), and the Gestapo (Secret State Police). The last-named had been in existence since 1933, several years before it was made a part of the RSHA, and for that reason was described in the Indictment separately from the other SS agencies. From 1935 until the end of the war it was headed by Heinrich Mueller, commonly called "Gestapo" Mueller.

Storey had presented the case against the Gestapo, and it certainly contained much evidence of terrible atrocities, especially in the German-occupied Eastern regions. In fact, many of the atrocities described by the prosecution involved a mingling of Gestapo, SD, and SIPO participants, and Storey's presentation did not always indicate the Gestapo's role in the crime.

There was little that the lawyer for the Gestapo, Dr. Rudolf Merkel, could do against the mass of really hellish evidence. . . .

In his final argument, Dr. Merkel spent little time on legal arguments and had the good sense not to dispute Gestapo crimes that were proven and notorious. He had some success in showing that there were many Gestapo members who had no part in the crimes. But Merkel put major emphasis on his final pages, pointing out particular sections of the Gestapo, including office employees, telephone operators, and other such categories, whom Justice Jackson had previously proposed to exempt from the Indictment. Merkel also mentioned administrative officials and technical employees whose work had nothing to do with police activities. Merkel concluded: "I have not considered it my duty to excuse crimes and evil deeds or to whitewash those who disregarded the laws of humanity. But I desire to save those who are innocent; I desire to clear the way for a sentence which will dethrone the powers of darkness and reconstitute the moral order of the world." . . .

Indicting the SS

In December 1945 Major Warren Farr had delivered a well-organized and forceful presentation of the prosecution's evidence against the SS, covering the concentration camps, persecution and extermination of the Jews, and involvement in preparations for aggressive war. This had taken less than a full day's session. But when, seven months later, Horst Pelckmann presented his defense of the SS against the charge that it was a criminal organization, the issues and evidence were so numerous and varied that more than five full days' sessions were required to complete the oral evidence, much to the Tribunal's annoyance. . . .

Pelckmann . . . turned his attention to the Waffen-SS, a fighting force which by the end of the war comprised some thirty-five divisions and approximately 550,000 men. It embodied from two-thirds to three-quarters of all members of the SS. Rightly or wrongly, the Waffen-SS acquired the reputation of spreading terror, not only among enemy troops but also among civilians. It was, surely, the horror spread by these half a million soldiers which moved Colonel Bernays to propose criminalization of the Nazi organizations, among which the Waffen-SS was the prime target.

The lawyers at Nuremberg were in general agreement that Article 9 of the Charter should not be applied to an organization unless most of its members had joined voluntarily. The prosecution had been proceeding on the basis that this was true of the Waffen-SS, although it was known that toward the end of the war some recruits had been forced to join. . . . During the war 320,000 casualties were suffered, the majority of whom were volunteers, and by the end of the war the Waffen-SS draftees somewhat outnumbered the surviving volunteers. . . .

The evidence clearly showed that many thousands of them had known of and been involved in war crimes, some of appalling evil. But could one say the same of hundreds of thousands? Pelckmann and his witnesses had raised the issue, and, in his way, he stated it in his conclusion:

> I indict every one of the murderers and criminals who belonged to that organization or one of its units—and there are more than a few of them.
>
> I acquit the thousands and hundreds of thousands of those who served in good faith, and who therefore share only morally and metaphysically, not criminally, the guilt which the German people must bitterly bear.
>
> But I warn the world and its judges against the commitment of mass injustice in legal form, against the creation of a mass of condemned and outlawed individuals in the heart of Europe; I warn so that the longing of all peoples and men may be fulfilled.

Going After the High Command

On August 9, 1946, Dr. Hans Laternser began his defense of the General Staff and High Command of the German Armed Forces, described in the indictment as "Functioning . . . in association as a group at a highest level in the German Armed Forces Organization" in violation of all four counts in the Indictment.

My own attitude toward the effort to bring this "group" within the ambit of Article 9 of the Charter had changed since I had stated the prosecution's case early in January. Up to that time, despite my doubts about the sufficiency of the "group's" definition and the legal validity of Article 9, I had proceeded on the basis that there was merit in Bernays's concern about the great multitude of probable war criminals, and my superiors had chosen this way of dealing with the problem—an attitude supported by the great volume of documentary material revealing much criminal activity by Germany's military leaders.

As previously described, for me the whole picture had been changed when General Clay launched the Denazification Program, under which the vast majority of Nazi organization members would be dealt with in German administrative proceedings or courts. Even more immediately important, it had become clear that the purpose Bernays had had in mind did not apply to the German Staff–High Command case (or the Reich Cabinet as well), which numbered only some 135 members who could best be dealt with in regular court proceedings. For enforcement of international penal law against the German military leaders the "organizational" procedure was quite unnecessary.

It now appeared to me, however, that Jackson wished (although he never said this to me) to fix the stigma of criminality on the German military leadership as a whole by the Tribunal's declaration. I had no right to abandon the course that Jackson had assigned me to take, and, furthermore, to drop the project would be regarded by many as a whitewash of the German leaders, which, in my view, they ill deserved. It was up to me to carry on, although I was by no means sanguine that the Tribunal would find that the General Staff as defined in the Indictment was a "group" within the meaning of Article 9 of the Charter. To me, the most important objective was to ensure that the result did not appear to be an exoneration of German military leadership.

As witnesses, Laternser called three field marshals: Walter von Brauchitsch, who had been Commander in Chief of the army from 1938 to his retirement late in 1941, and Erich von Manstein and Gerd von Rundstedt, both renowned commanders of Army Groups. . . .

When I cross-examined Manstein, I had concluded that fencing with him about the "group" would be playing from weakness and that his vulnerable spot was the Einsatzgruppen [execution squads sent into conquered parts of Eastern Europe to eliminate Jews and other undesirables], redolent as they were with atrocious murders on a vast scale. I did not for a moment believe Manstein's claim that he knew nothing of the massacres. I did not expect to make him confess his knowledge, but rather to show how absurd it was to suppose that murder groups moved through the army's front and rear lines without being noticed or that an alert commander would not want to know what these unusual armed units sponsored by Himmler were doing.

I thought I made some headway, but my "luck" consisted of a new document . . . in which Manstein was shown to have distributed to his troops an anti-Jewish manifesto that closely resembled one which Field Marshal von Reichenau had issued on October 10, 1941, and which I had offered in evidence in January. I asked Manstein what he had done when Hitler had sent him the Reichenau manifesto "as a model." He replied: "I did nothing about it and I considered such an order as quite beside the point, because I wanted to conduct the fight in a military manner and in no other way."

I then offered in evidence the new document of November 20, 1941, signed by Manstein, which read in part:

> Since 22 June the German people have been engaged in a life-and-death struggle against the Bolshevist system.

This struggle is not being carried out against the Soviet Armed forces alone in the established form laid down by European rules of warfare. . . .

The Jewish-Bolshevist system must be exterminated once and for all. Never again must it encroach on our European living space.

The German soldier has not only the task of crushing the military potential of this system. He comes also as the bearer of a racial concept and as the avenger of all the cruelties which have been perpetrated on him and on the German people. . . .

The soldier must appreciate the necessity for the harsh punishment of Jewry, the spiritual bearer of the Bolshevist-terror. This is also necessary in order to nip in the bud all uprisings which are mostly plotted by Jews.

Manstein feebly insisted that he could not remember this document, but admitted that he had signed it. His credibility was shattered. . . .

Cross-examining Rundstedt, [prosecutor Peter] Calvocoressi endeavored to bolster the "group" by forcing Rundstedt to acknowledge a gathering of the leading generals in August 1938 seeking to unite in opposition to making war against Czechoslovakia. But Peter had no such potent document [like the one that exposed Manstein].

As was to be expected, Laternser's closing argument was excellent with regard to the "group" issue. But his handling of the criminal aspects of the prosecution's charges was seriously marred by his repeated disregard of the defense's difficulties. For example, while Laternser was able to declare with considerable validity that the annexation of Austria and the Sudetenland had not been aggressive wars and would not necessarily have alerted the generals to Hitler's aggrandizing intentions, the same could certainly not be said of the domination and virtual annexation of the rest of Czechoslovakia in March 1939. Laternser brushed it off as a "purely political action" and, to be sure, there was no fighting. But to call this a "peaceful entry" was no way to describe a bitter yielding to the mandate of vastly superior forces and threats to destroy the country. Here was no ethnic factor such as gave some shred of validity to the Sudeten claims; here was only a crass seizure of the lands and peoples of another country in flagrant violation of agreements freshly made with Britain, France, and Italy. This was the trigger of [British prime minister] Neville Chamberlain's final awakening to Hitler's real intentions, and what he saw, the German generals could also see. . . .

The Cabinet and the SA

The last two organizations charged were the Reich Cabinet (Reichsregierung) and the Sturmabteilung of the Nazi Party, commonly known as the SA. The Reich Cabinet had at least as frail a claim as the General Staff to be accredited as an Article 9 "organization" or "group." The SA, on the other hand, had less difficulty on that score, but its loss of prestige in consequence of the 1934 Roehm purge and its very secondary status during the war raised doubt of its sufficient importance to warrant the charges. . . .

Better remembered in America and England as the "Brownshirts," the SA was highly visible, in press and film, as the Nazi street gangs who fought Communists and other rival parties and factions and harassed Jews. It was, no doubt, these recollections and unawareness of what had followed that led the chief prosecutors to include the SA among the indicted organizations. But that aspect of the Nazi scene faded away as Hitler succeeded in crushing organized opposition and then destroyed the SA's leadership in the Roehm purge. . . .

[British prosecutor Sir David Maxwell-] Fyfe began with accusations that the SA had been involved in atrocities against the people of the German-occupied Eastern areas. [Defense witness Max] Juettner admitted that an SA unit had "on instructions from the Wehrmacht, transported prisoners of war to the rear during the Polish campaign" and that the SA had established bases in the Polish areas annexed by Germany and in the Government-General. These facts might be of use to the prosecution as showing the SA engaging in aggressive war, but were not in themselves criminal. And Juettner vehemently denied Fyfe's accusations that the SA had any bases or activities in Lithuania or had participated in atrocities there or anywhere else. The cross-examination soon turned into a running battle between accusation and denial in which it was hard for the listener to form an opinion. . . .

Final Arguments

And so, near the end of the Tribunal's session on August 28, 1946, the defense lawyers finished their last pleas. It was now time for the prosecution's final arguments, and Fyfe led off with what was to be much the longest of these efforts.

Fyfe informed the Tribunal that he would cover the Party Political Leaders, the SA, and the SS; these were, of course, the largest chunks of the prosecution's case against the organizations. He began with a short attack on [the defense] against Article 9 of the Charter. However, instead of using legal arguments, Fyfe resorted to political and evidentiary factors. Many of the organizational criminals were still at large in Germany, said Fyfe, and they should not "be set loose among the German people and amongst the people of Europe."

Fyfe then leveled an almost brutal attack on the defendants' evidence:

> On the face of it, the evidence which has been given by almost all the witnesses called before your Commissioners is untrue. You yourselves [i.e., the Tribunal] have seen and heard some of these witnesses, selected by defense counsel presumably because they were thought to be the most reliable. . . . Their evidence is no better.

Fyfe then named [several defense witnesses] as especially fork-tongued and concluded:

> The evidence of all of them is the same. They are asked if they knew of the persecution and annihilation of the Jews, of the dread works of the Gestapo, of the atrocities within the concentration camps, of the ill-treatment of slave labor, of the intention and prepa-

ration to wage aggressive war, of the murder of brave soldiers, sailors, and airmen. And they reply with "the everlasting No."

The effect on the Tribunal of this frontal attack is not clear. No doubt there was a lot of mendacity among the witnesses, but I saw no basis for such an across-the-board attack and, judging by the results, neither did the Tribunal. . . .

To incriminate the Leadership Corps, Fyfe had put together documents and selections of testimony involving the leaders in wartime atrocities against Jews, slave labor, euthanasia, mass mistreatment and killing of Soviet prisoners of war, and unlawful treatment of enemy aviators forced down in German-occupied territory.

Although he made no admission of difficulty, Fyfe was well aware that the SA posed much more difficult problems than the Leadership Corps, and he immediately tackled the defense's contention of involuntary membership. . . .

Fyfe succeeded admirably in portraying the SA as riddled with violent crime on the streets and in the early concentration camps such as Oranienburg, where the SA officer Werner Schaefer had been the first Commandant. After the Roehm purge, little street fighting remained for the SA, but, as Fyfe put it: "The Church and the Jews remained an ever present problem." All this helped to paint the SA as an evil enterprise, but the prosecution's legal difficulty was that prewar sins, however criminal and disgusting, were not war crimes, and were thus outside the reach of Article 6 of the Charter.

Fyfe made an effort to show SA "preparation for war and wartime activities," but he had pitifully little evidence to cite. Ingenuously, Fyfe declared: "The crimes of the SA did not end with the outbreak of war." He might more accurately have said that the SA's crimes began with the coming of war, for the international laws of war then came into play. Then, at least, the SA's activities in German-annexed and -occupied Poland appeared to have produced a small but shocking body of evidence. Whatever exaggerations or mistakes might be found in the affidavits on which Fyfe relied, he made no mention of them.

The SS, the last of Fyfe's group, posed no such problems, and he informed the Tribunal that he "did not conceive to be necessary to deal at any length with the evidence against the SS.". . .

Fyfe had covered the Organization charges so completely that Tom Dodd, who presented the major argument for the United States, had very little fresh ground left for him. I had expected Dodd to focus on the Reich Cabinet, Gestapo, and SD, which Fyfe had handled only cursorily. Instead, Dodd proceeded to cover all of the organizations except the General Staff–High Command.

Dodd's text was well put together, but it was really a compendium of the prosecution's evidence, all of which was by that time well known to the Tribunal and the court lawyers and staff. It therefore appeared to me that Dodd was offering his swan song not so much to the Tribunal as to the world outside, and especially to the American public. Only at the end did Dodd turn to the legal questions about Article 9, and then he swept away the defendants' arguments rather cavalierly, and extolled the importance of the case against the organizations:

> By a declaration of criminality against these organizations, this Tribunal will put on notice not only the people of Germany but the people of the whole world. Mankind will know that no crime will go unpunished because it was committed in the name of a political party or of a state; that no crime will be passed by because it is too big; that no criminal will avoid punishment because there are too many.

The last clause did indeed embody the purpose which had moved Murray Bernays to propose the organization charges. But by the end of the trial it had become apparent to most of us that such thorough police and court work was most unlikely.

The Cross-Examination of Hermann Göring

Robert H. Jackson

For much of the Nazi reign of terror Hermann Göring was the most powerful man in Germany other than Adolf Hitler. Over the course of his political career he was responsible for many of the key elements of the regime. He was, for example, the president of the Reichstag, the German parliament, chief of the secret police, and the commander of the air force. Until he had a falling out with Hitler toward the end of the war, he was the Führer's chosen successor. However, in his capacity as head of the air force, Göring saw his early war successes reversed later in the war and the Luftwaffe's offensive failures in the east, coupled with its inability to defend Germany against Allied attacks, led to a gradual lack of influence. Within Hitler's inner circle of advisers, Göring was ultimately outmaneuvered by others, including Martin Bormann and Heinrich Himmler, and lost Hitler's support. In the last months of the war, he was stripped of all his titles, expelled from the Party and arrested. To Allied prosecutors, however, Göring was the highest rank-ing official among the defendants, and also one of the most intelligent and unrepentant. In a dramatic courtroom con-frontation, chief prosecutor Robert H. Jackson cross-examined Göring. Many observers felt Göring got the best of Jackson, but it made no difference in the verdict. This excerpt provides a flavor of the exchange and focuses on Göring's part in the

Excerpted from Robert H. Jackson's cross-examination of Hermann Göring, as recorded in *The Nurnberg Case as Presented by Robert H. Jackson* (New York: Knopf, 1947).

I elimination of Jews from Germany's economy, the first steps toward the eventual genocide of the Holocaust.

Jackson. Now, I want to review with you briefly what the prosecution understands to be public acts taken by you in reference to the Jewish question. From the very beginning you regarded the elimination of the Jew from the economic life of Germany as one phase of the Four Year Plan under your jurisdiction, did you not?

Göring. The elimination, yes; that is right in part. The elimination as far as the large concerns were concerned because there continually disturbances were created by pointing out that there were large industries, also armament industries, still under Jewish directors or with Jewish shareholders, and that caused serious disturbances about the industries.

Jackson. Do I understand that you want the Tribunal to believe that all you were concerned about was the big Jewish enterprises? That is the way you want to be understood?

Göring. I was not at first disturbed by the small stores.

Jackson. When did you become disturbed with the small stores?

Göring. When trade had to be limited, then it was pointed out that this could be done first by closing the Jewish stores.

Public Acts Against the Jews

Jackson. Now, let us go through the public acts which you performed on the Jewish question. First, did you proclaim the Nürnberg racial laws?

Göring. As President of the Reichstag, yes; I have already stated that.

Jackson. What date was that?

Göring. 1935, I believe, in Nürnberg in September.

Jackson. That was the beginning of the legal measures taken against the Jews, was it not?

Göring. No, I believe that the elimination from various phases of civil employment was before. I could not state the exact date, but I believe that happened in 1933.

Jackson. Then on the first day of December 1936, you promulgated an act making a death penalty for Germans to transfer property abroad or leave it abroad; the property of a culprit to be forfeited to the state, and the "People's Court" given jurisdiction of such cases, did you not?

Göring. That is correct, the act to protect foreign currency. That is to say, whoever without the permission of the government established an account in a foreign country.

Jackson. Then, your third public act was on April 22, 1939, when you published penalties for veiling the character of a Jewish enterprise within the Reich, was it not?

Göring. Yes.

Jackson. Then on July 28, 1939, you published certain

There Must Be a Law

Though no trial like Nuremberg had ever been held to determine the criminality of actions taken by officials during a war, legal precedents did exist for prosecuting the Germans for some of their crimes. Existing international law was not adequate, however, for addressing all of the Nazis' misdeeds, particularly the atrocities committed against civilians, especially the Jews. This excerpt by political scientist Heinz Eulau explains why Nuremberg introduced a new offense, Crimes Against Humanity.

It has been our experience with the Nazi regime that racial, religious and political persecution by a government against its own people can reach such dimensions as to constitute a danger to the world community. As the indictment shows, the persecution of the Jews in Germany, the destruction of German trade unions, the liquidation of opposition parties, the attacks on the churches, etc., all paved the way to foreign aggression. It is true that these actions are not yet punishable by international law. But it is a matter of common sense that some law should be evolved to punish them. It is for this reason that Article 6 (C) of the Tribunal's charter grants jurisdiction over crimes against humanity—

prescriptions on the competence of the regular courts to handle those matters?

Göring. Please, would you kindly read the law to me? I do not know it.

Jackson. I will not take time reading it. Do you deny that you published *Reichsgesetzblatt* Law, 1939, found on page 1370, referring to the competence of the courts to handle penalties against the law? If you do not remember, say so.

Göring. Yes, I say that I cannot remember the law. If it was in the *Reichsgesetzblatt* and has my name under it, then, of course, it is so, but I do not remember the contents.

Jackson. On April 26, 1938, you, under the Four Year Plan, published a decree providing for the registration of Jewish property which provided that Jews inside and out-

---

"murder, extermination, enslavement, deportation and other inhumane acts committed against any civilian population, *before* or during the war; or persecutions on political, racial or religious grounds in execution of, or in connection with, any crime within the jurisdiction of the Tribunal, *whether or not in violation of the domestic law of the country where perpetrated.*"

The last (italicized) provision is important because it includes crimes committed within Germany against Germans even before the war. The principle has already been used at the recent Dachau trials. And the indictment specifies the charges made in this connection. It is pointed out that the Nazi criminals imprisoned opponents without judicial process, held them in concentration camps and subjected them to outrages. It mentions specifically the murder of the Social Democrat Breitscheid and the Communist Thaelmann, and the imprisonment of Pastor Niemoller. And it accuses the Nazi criminals of the confiscation of property of hundreds of thousands of Jews. If the Tribunal acts on these charges, a new conception of the extent of a state's internal sovereignty will enter international law.

Heinz Eulau, "The Nuremberg War-Crimes Trial," *New Republic*, November 12, 1945.

side Germany must register their property, did you not?

Göring. I assume so. I do not remember it any more, but if you have the decree there and if it is signed by me, there cannot be any doubt.

Jackson. On April 26, 1938, you published a decree under the Four Year Plan, did you not, that all acts of disposal of Jewish enterprises required the permission of the authorities?

Göring. That I remember.

Jackson. Then you published on November 12, 1938, a decree also under the Four Year Plan, imposing a fine of a billion marks for atonement on all Jews?

Göring. I have already explained that, that all the decrees of that time were signed by me, and I assumed responsibility for them.

Jackson. Then on November 12, 1938, you also signed a decree that, under the Four Year Plan, all damage caused to Jewish property by the riots of 1938 must be repaired immediately by the Jews, and at their own expense, and their insurance claims were forfeited to the Reich. Did you personally sign that law?

Göring. A similar law I signed. Whether it was exactly the same as you have just read, I could not say.

Jackson. You agree that that was the substance of the law, do you?

Göring. Yes.

Jackson. And on November 12, 1938, did you not also personally sign a decree, also under the Four Year Plan, that Jews may not own retail stores or engage independently in handicrafts or offer goods or services for sale at markets, fairs, or exhibitions, or be leaders of enterprises or members of co-operatives. Do you recall all of that?

Göring. Yes. These are all parts of the decrees for the elimination of Jewry from economic life.

Jackson. On February 21, 1939, you personally signed a decree, did you not, that the Jews must surrender all precious metals and jewels to a public officer within two weeks?

Göring. I do not remember that, but I am sure, without doubt, that that is correct.

Jackson. Did you not also, on March 3, 1939, sign a further decree concerning the period within which items of jewelry must be surrendered by Jews—*Reichsgesetzblatt,* Volume I, 1939, page 387?

Göring. I assume that was the decree of execution concerning the decree mentioned before. A law sometimes requires regulations of execution as a consequence of the law. Seen together, this is just one measure.

Jackson. Did you not also sign personally a decree on September 17, 1940, ordering the sequestration of Jewish property in Poland?

Göring. Yes. I stated that once before. In that part of Poland, if I may point that out, which had been previously an old German province. It was to return to Germany.

Jackson. Did you not also, on November 30, 1940, personally, in the capacity of President of the Reich Defense Council, sign a decree which provided that the Jews should receive no compensation for damages caused by enemy attacks or by German Forces? I refer to *Reichsgesetzblatt,* Volume I, 1940, page 1547.

Göring. If you have it there before you, then it must be correct.

Jackson. You have no recollection of that?

Göring. Not concerning all details of law and decrees. That is impossible.

Toward the Final Solution

Jackson. Then it was you, was it not, who signed, on July 31, 1941, a decree asking [Heinrich] Himmler and the chief of security police and the SS *Gruppenführer* [Reinhard] Heydrich to make the plans for the complete solution of the Jewish question?

Göring. No, that is not correct. This decree I know very well.

Jackson. I ask to have you shown document 710–PS, US–509.

(A document was handed to the witness)
That document is signed by you, is it not?

Göring. That is correct.

Jackson. And it is addressed to the chief of the security police and the security service and to SS *Gruppenführer* Heydrich, isn't it?

Göring. That is also correct.

Jackson. That we may have no difficulty about the translation of this, you correct me if I am wrong:

Completing the task that was assigned to you on January 24, 1939—

Göring. That is a mistake already. It says

In completion of the task which has been transferred to you, not as it was translated to me before.

Jackson. Very well, I will accept that.

Which dealt with arriving at, through furtherance of emigration and evacuation, a solution of the Jewish problem, as advantageous as possible, I hereby charge you with making all necessary preparations in regard to organizational and financial matters for bringing about a complete solution of the Jewish question in the German sphere of influence in Europe.

Am I correct so far?

Göring. No, that is in no way correctly translated into the German.

Jackson. Give us your translation of it.

Göring. May I read it as it is written here?

In completion of the task which has been conferred upon you already on the 24th, 1939, to solve the Jewish problem in the form of emigration and evacuation and to bring to the best possible solution, according to present conditions, I charge you herewith to make all necessary preparations in the way of organization and material matters.

Now comes the decisive word which has been mistranslated:

For a collective solution,
not

for a final solution—

For an entire, a collective solution of the Jewish question within the area of German influence in Europe. As far as here the competency of other agencies would be touched, they are to participate. I charge you further to submit to me soon your total plan concerning it in the way of organization and materials, in order to be able to carry out the desired solution of the Jewish question, in completing the task which has been turned over to you on January 24, 1939.

That is to say, at a time when no war had started or was to be expected. . . .

[Göring goes on to answer questions about riots that broke out on November 9 and 10 in which German Party members destroyed Jewish-owned businesses in Berlin. The rampage was known as Kristallnacht, "the night of broken glass."]

Jackson. After the riot of November 9 and 10, you have testified that you called a meeting on November 12 and ordered all officials concerned to be present, and that the Führer had insisted on Goebbels being present?

Göring. Yes. . . .

Jackson. This is the meeting held on November 12, 1938, at the office of the Reich Ministry for Air. That is correct, is it not?

Göring. Yes, that is correct.

Jackson. You opened the meeting:

Gentlemen, today's meeting is of a decisive nature. I have received a letter written on the Führer's orders by the Stabsleiter of the Führer's Deputy Bormann, requesting that the Jewish question be now, once for all, co-ordinated and solved one way or another.

Is that correct?

Göring. Yes, that is correct.

Jackson. Further down, I find this by you:

Because, gentlemen, I have had enough of these demonstrations. They don't harm the Jews, but me, who is the last authority for co-ordinating the German economy. If today a Jewish shop is destroyed, if goods are thrown into the street, the insurance company will pay for the damages which the Jew does not even have, and furthermore, goods of the consumer, goods belonging to the people, are destroyed. If, in the future, demonstrations which are necessary occur, then I pray that they be directed so as not to hurt us.

Am I correct?

Göring. Yes, quite correct.

Jackson. Skipping two or three paragraphs, I come to this—

I shouldn't want to leave any doubt, gentlemen, as to the aim of today's meeting. We have not come together merely to talk again, but to make decisions, and I implore the competent agencies to take all measures for the elimination of the Jew from German economy and to submit them to me as far as is necessary.

Göring. That is correct. . . .

Eliminating Jews from All Positions in Public Life

Jackson. You then take up at considerable length the method by which you shall Aryanize Jewish stores, is that right?

Göring. Yes.

Jackson. And then you take up the Aryanization of Jewish factories?

Göring. Yes.

Jackson. You take up the smaller factories first?

Göring. Yes.

Jackson. Quoting:

As for the smaller and medium ones, two things shall have to be made clear: First, which factories do I not need at all, which are the ones where production could be suspended? Could they not be put to another use? If not, the factories will be razed immediately.

Second, in case the factory should be needed, it will be turned over to Aryans in the same manner as the stores.

That is correct, is it?

Göring. Yes. . . .

Jackson. Then Dr. Goebbels raised the question of Jews traveling on railway trains?

Göring. Yes.

Jackson. And see if I quote the dialogue between you and Dr. Goebbels correctly on that subject. That Dr. Goebbels said:

Furthermore, I advocate that Jews be eliminated from all positions in public life in which they may prove to be provocative. It is still possible today that a Jew shares a compartment in a sleeping car with a German; therefore, we need a decree by the Reich Ministry for Communications stating that separate compartments for Jews shall be available. In cases where compartments are filled up, Jews cannot claim a seat. They shall be given separate compartments only after all Germans have secured seats. They shall not mix with the Germans, and if there is no more room, they shall have to stand in the corridor.

Is that right?
Göring. Yes, that is correct.
Jackson.

Göring: In that case I think it would make more sense to give them separate compartments. Goebbels: Not if the train is overcrowded. Göring: Just a moment. There will be only one Jewish coach. If that is filled up the other Jews will have to stay at home. Goebbels: Suppose though there won't be many Jews going on an express train to Munich. Suppose there will be two Jews in a train, and the other compartments would be overcrowded; those two Jews would then have a compartment all by themselves; therefore, Jews may claim a seat only after all Germans have secured a seat. Göring: I would give the Jews one coach, or one compartment, and should a case like you mentioned arise, and the train be overcrowded, believe me, we won't need a law. We will kick him out, and he will have to sit alone in the toilet all the way.

Is that correct?
Göring. Yes. I had become a little nervous when Goebbels had had important matters that were brought forward in certain particulars, and in this connection I gave out no decrees or no laws. Of course, today it is very pleasant for the prosecution to present it, but I wish to state that it was a very lively session, in which Goebbels made demands which were as I say in a radical scope, and in a radical criminal scope, and in accordance with my demeanor I expressed myself.

The Cross-Examination of Albert Speer

Robert H. Jackson

Albert Speer was Hitler's chief architect and minister for armaments and war production. In the former position he was tasked with rebuilding Berlin, but his grandiose vision was never realized. He did, however, design the parade grounds, searchlights, and banners used in the Nuremberg party congress of 1934. In 1942, Speer became minister of armaments and munitions and later became responsible for all war production. In this position, he made extensive use of slave laborers taken from concentration camps to produce material for Germany's war effort. A confidant of Hitler for most of the war, Speer lost favor when he refused to carry out the Führer's order to destroy German installations that were about to be captured by the Allies late in the war. Unlike his co-defendants on trial, Speer acknowledged his guilt and this undoubtedly led the justices to give him the relatively lenient sentence of twenty years imprisonment. After being released from Spandau prison in West Berlin in 1966, Speer wrote a number of books, most notably a memoir of his role during the war. In this excerpt from the proceedings at Nuremberg, prosecutor Robert H. Jackson elicits from Speer an explanation of his role in employing concentration camp prisoners as slave laborers.

Excerpted from Robert H. Jackson's cross-examination of Albert Speer, as recorded by the Avalon Project: *Nuremberg Trial Proceedings*, vol. 16, at www.yale.edu/lawweb/avalon/ imt/proc/06-21-46.htm.

JUSTICE JACKSON: Now there has been some testimony about your relation to concentration camps, and, as I understand it, you have said to us that you did use and encourage the use of forced labor from the concentration camps.

SPEER: Yes, we did use it in the German armament industry.

JUSTICE JACKSON: And I think you also recommended that persons in labor camps who were slackers be sent to the concentration camps, did you not?

SPEER: That was the question of the so-called "Bummelanten," and by that name we meant workers who did not get to their work on time or who pretended to be ill. Severe measures were taken against such workers during the war, and I approved of these measures.

JUSTICE JACKSON: In fact, in the 30 October 1942 meeting of the Central Planning Board you brought the subject up in the following terms, did you not—quoting Speer:

". . . There is nothing to be said against SS and Police taking drastic steps and putting those known to be slackers into concentration camp factories. There is no alternative. Let it happen several times, and the news will soon get around."

That was your recommendation?

SPEER: Correct.

JUSTICE JACKSON: In other words, the workmen stood in considerable terror of concentration camps, and you wanted to take advantage of that to keep them at their work, did you not?

SPEER: It is certain that concentration camps had a bad reputation with us, and the transfer to a concentration camp, or threat of such a possibility, was bound to reduce the number of absentees in the factories right from the beginning. But at that meeting, as I already said yesterday, there was nothing further said about it. It was one of the many remarks one can make in wartime when one is upset.

JUSTICE JACKSON: However, it is very clear—and if I misinterpret you I give you the chance to correct me—that you understood the very bad reputation that the concentration camps had among the workmen and that the concentration camps were regarded as being much more severe than the labor camps as places to be in.

SPEER: That is correct. I knew that. I did not know, of course, what I have heard during this trial, but the other thing was a generally known fact.

JUSTICE JACKSON: Well, it was known throughout Germany, was it not, that the concentration camps were pretty tough places to be put?

SPEER: Yes, but not to the extent which has been revealed in this trial.

JUSTICE JACKSON: And the bad reputation of the concentration camp, as a matter of fact, was a part of its usefulness in making people fearful of being sent there, was it not?

SPEER: No doubt concentration camps were a means, a menace used to keep order.

JUSTICE JACKSON: And to keep people at work?

SPEER: I would not like to put it in that way. I assert that a great number of the foreign workers in our country did their work quite voluntarily once they had come to Germany.

Labor Agreement

JUSTICE JACKSON: Well, we will take that up later. You used the concentration camp labor in production to the extent that you were required to divide the proceeds of the labor with [SS chief Heinrich] Himmler, did you not?

SPEER: That I did not understand.

JUSTICE JACKSON: Well, you made an agreement finally with Himmler that he should have 5 percent, or roughly 5 percent, of the production of the concentration camp labor while you would get for your work 95 percent?

SPEER: No, that is not quite true.

JUSTICE JACKSON: Well, tell me how it was. That is what the documents indicate, if I read them aright.

SPEER: Yes, it is put that way in the Fuehrer minutes [notes from a staff meeting], but I should like to explain the meaning to you. Himmler, as I said yesterday, wanted to build factories of his own in his concentration camps. Then he would have been able to produce arms without any outside control, which Hitler, of course, knew. The 5 percent arms production which was to have been handed to Himmler was to a certain extent a compensation for the fact that he himself gave up the idea of building factories in the camps. From the psychological point of view it was not so simple for me to get Himmler to give up this idea when he kept on reminding Hitler of it. I was hoping that he would be satisfied with the 5 percent arms production we were going to give him. Actually this 5 percent was never handed over. We managed things quietly with the Operations Staff of the OKW and with General Buhle, so that he never got the arms at all.

JUSTICE JACKSON: Well, I am not criticizing the bargain, you understand. I don't doubt you did very well to get 95 percent, but the point is that Himmler was using, with your knowledge, concentration camp labor to manufacture arms, or was proposing to do so, and you wanted to keep that production within your control?

SPEER: Could the translation come through a bit clearer? Would you please repeat that?

JUSTICE JACKSON: You knew at this time that Himmler was using concentration camp labor to carry on independent industry and that he proposed to go into the armament industry in order to have a source of supply of arms for his own SS?

SPEER: Yes.

The Jewish Question

JUSTICE JACKSON: You also knew the policy of the Nazi Party and the policy of the Government towards the Jews, did you not?

SPEER: I knew that the National Socialist Party was anti-Semitic, and I knew that the Jews were being evacuated from Germany.

JUSTICE JACKSON: In fact, you participated in that evacuation, did you not?

SPEER: No.

JUSTICE JACKSON: Well, I gather that impression from Document L-156, Exhibit RF-1522, a letter from the Plenipotentiary for the Allocation of Labor which is dated 26 March 1943, which you have no doubt seen. You may see it again, if you wish. In which he says. . .

SPEER: I know it.

JUSTICE JACKSON: "At the end of February, the Reichsfuehrer SS, in agreement with myself and the Reich Minister for armaments and munitions, for reasons of state security, has removed from their places of work all Jews who were still working freely and not in camps, and either transferred them to a labor corps or collected them for removal."

Was that a correct representation of your activity?

SPEER: No.

JUSTICE JACKSON: Will you tell me what part you had in that? There is no question that they were put into labor corps or collected for removal, is there?

SPEER: That is correct.

JUSTICE JACKSON: Now you say you did not do it, so will you tell me who did?

SPEER: It was a fairly long business. When, in February 1942, I took over my new office, the Party was already insisting that Jews who were still working in armament factories should be removed from them. I objected at the time, and managed to get [Hitler's secretary Martin] Bormann to issue a circular letter to the effect that these Jews might go on being employed in armament factories and that Party offices were prohibited from accusing the heads of these firms on political grounds because of the Jews working there. It was the Gauleiter who made such political accusations against the heads of concerns, and it was mostly in the Gau Saxony and in the Gau Berlin. So after this the Jews could remain in these plants.

Without having any authority to do so, I had had this circular letter from the Party published in my news sheet to heads of factories and had sent it to all concerned, so that I would in any case receive their complaints if the Party should not obey the instruction. After that the problem was left alone, until September or October of 1942. At that time a conference with Hitler took place, at which [labor leader Fritz] Sauckel also was present. At this conference Hitler insisted emphatically that the Jews must now be removed from the armament firms, and he gave orders for this to be done—this will be seen from a Fuehrer protocol which has been preserved. In spite of this we managed to keep the Jews on in factories and it was only in March 1943, as this letter shows, that resistance gave way and the Jews finally did have to get out.

I must point out to you that, as far as I can remember, it was not yet a question of the Jewish problem as a whole, but in the years 1941 and 1942 Jews had gone to the armament factories to do important war work and have an occupation of military importance; they were able to escape the evacuation which at that time was already in full swing. They were mostly occupied in the electrical industry, and Geheimrat Bucher, of the electrical industry—that is AEG and Siemens—no doubt lent a helping hand in order to get the Jews taken on there in greater numbers. These Jews were completely free and their families were still in their homes.

The letter by Gauleiter Sauckel you have before you was not, of course, submitted to me; and Sauckel says that he himself had not seen it. But it is certainly true that I knew about it before action was taken; I knew because the question had to be discussed as to how one should get replacements. It is equally certain, though, that I also protested at the time at having skilled labor removed from my armament industries because, apart from other reasons, it was going to make things difficult for me.

The War Effort

JUSTICE JACKSON: That is exactly the point that I want to emphasize. As I understand it, you were struggling to get manpower enough to produce the armaments to win a war for Germany.

SPEER: Yes.

JUSTICE JACKSON: And this anti-Semitic campaign was so strong that it took trained technicians away from you and disabled you from performing your functions. Now, isn't that the fact?

SPEER: I did not understand the meaning of your question.

JUSTICE JACKSON: Your problem of creating armaments to win the war for Germany was made very much more difficult by this anti-Jewish campaign which was being waged by others of your codefendants.

SPEER: That is a certainty; and it is equally clear that if the Jews who were evacuated had been allowed to work for me, it would have been a considerable advantage to me. . . .

JUSTICE JACKSON: Now I want to ask you about the recruiting of forced labor. As I understand it, you know about the deportation of 100,000 Jews from Hungary for subterranean airplane factories, and you told us in your interrogation of 18 October 1945 that you made no objection to it. That is true, is it not?

SPEER: That is true, yes.

JUSTICE JACKSON: And you told us also, quite candidly, on that day that it was no secret to you that a good deal of the manpower . . . was brought in by illegal methods. That is also true, is it not?

SPEER: I took great care at the time to notice what expression the interrogating officer used; he used the expression "they came against their wish"; and that I confirmed.

JUSTICE JACKSON: Did you not say that it was no secret to you that they were brought in an illegal manner? Didn't you add that yourself?

SPEER: No, no. That was certainly not so.

JUSTICE JACKSON: Well, in any event, you knew that at the Fuehrer conference in August of 1942 the Fuehrer had approved of all coercive measures for obtaining labor if they couldn't be obtained on a voluntary basis, and you knew that that program was carried out. You, as a matter of fact, you did not give any particular attention to the legal side of this thing, did you? You were after manpower; isn't that the fact?

SPEER: That is absolutely correct.

JUSTICE JACKSON: And whether it was legal or illegal was not your worry?

SPEER: I consider that in view of the whole war situation and of our views in general on this question it was justified.

JUSTICE JACKSON: Yes, it was in accordance with the policy of the Government, and that was as far as you inquired at the time, was it not?

SPEER: Yes. I am of the opinion that at the time I took over my office, in February 1942, all the violations of international law, which later—which are now brought up against me, had already been committed.

JUSTICE JACKSON: And you don't question that you share a certain responsibility for that program for bringing in— whether it is a legal responsibility or not, in fact—for bringing in this labor against its will? You don't deny that, do you?

SPEER: The workers were brought to Germany largely against their will, and I had no objection to their being brought to Germany against their will. On the contrary, during the first period, until the autumn of 1942, I certainly also took some pains to see that as many workers as possible should be brought to Germany in this manner.

Chapter 3

The Challenge of Being Fair

Chapter Preface

M any critics of the Nuremberg Trial contend that the final judgment was a foregone conclusion before the proceedings began. Since the Allies were victorious, they held power over the vanquished, and any claim of justice being served was merely a mask for vengeance. Yet the Allies could have skipped a trial altogether, as British prime minister Winston Churchill and Soviet premier Joseph Stalin preferred, and simply executed the Nazis they held responsible for the war. In the end, however, the Allies recognized that all was not fair in the treatment of a vanquished enemy and that a trial would help highlight the difference between their governments and that of Germany, which had allowed no legal recourse for the millions of displaced or murdered civilians that the Nazis had deemed the scourge of the Reich.

Trials are never perfect, and the Nuremberg Trial was no exception. Still, it has stood the test of time as an example of a criminal prosecution that was conducted with about as much impartiality as possible. Critics at the time understandably questioned how nations that had suffered so greatly at the hands of the Nazis could objectively judge their actions. There was no real alternative, however, and even in more conventional trials the same questions could be asked. After all, a person suspected of treason is always tried by the country he or she spied against. Neutral judges are not called in. An accused thief cannot complain of being treated unfairly because the jury is composed of honest people.

Still, the Allies grappled with the issues related to ensuring that the accused were given fair treatment and that the trial was conducted in an open fashion. But this did not stop legal experts and pundits alike from pointing out the potential for abuses of power in a trial that seemed likely to have but one possible outcome.

Setting Dangerous Legal Precedents

Charles E. Wyzanski Jr.

In the following article written at the time of the trial, U.S. District Court judge Charles E. Wyzanski Jr. considers the implications of the justice decided upon and meted out at Nuremberg. Wyzanski was a judge in Massachusetts not affiliated with the proceedings, but like all legal scholars he was concerned with the decisions of the trial. As Wyzanski points out, the indictments against the German defendants are often not based on legal precedent because there had never before been an international tribunal charged with the duty of trying war criminals. The crime of "waging an aggressive war," for example, had been previously leveled at entire nations, but at Nuremberg it was individual Germans who were accused of violating this law. To hold individual participants guilty of crimes of the state, in Wyzanski's view, is unprecedented. Furthermore, Wyzanski notes that the actions of many nations, including the Allied countries, places in doubt the sincerity of a belief that waging a war of aggression is a crime in international affairs. Although Wyzanski does not excuse the heinous acts of the Nazis, he does fear that creating laws to judge their deeds may set dangerous precedents for future law. He voices the concern that the trial is motivated by politics rather than justice, and that any decisions handed down in the court may come back to haunt citizens in the supposedly democratic nations that stand in judgment.

Excerpted from "Nuremberg: A Fair Trial? Dangerous Precedent," by Charles E. Wyzanski Jr., *The Atlantic Monthly*, April 1946.

The Nuremberg War Trial has a strong claim to be considered the most significant as well as the most debatable event since the conclusion of hostilities. To those who support the trial it promises the first effective recognition of a world law for the punishment of malefactors who start wars or conduct them in bestial fashion. To the adverse critics the trial appears in many aspects a negation of principles which they regard as the heart of any system of justice under law.

This sharp division of opinion has not been fully aired largely because it relates to an issue of foreign policy upon which this nation has already acted and on which debate may seem useless or, worse, merely to impair this country's prestige and power abroad. Moreover, to the casual newspaper reader the long-range implications of the trial are not obvious. He sees most clearly that there are in the dock a score of widely known men who plainly deserve punishment. And he is pleased to note that four victorious nations, who have not been unanimous on all post-war questions, have, by a miracle of administrative skill, united in a proceeding that is overcoming the obstacles of varied languages, professional habits, and legal traditions. But the more profound observer is aware that the foundations of the Nuremberg trial may mark a watershed of modern law.

Before I come to the discussion of the legal and political questions involved, let me make it clear that nothing I may say about the Nuremberg trial should be construed as a suggestion that the individual Nuremberg defendants or others who have done grievous wrongs should be set at liberty. In my opinion there are valid reasons why several thousand Germans, including many defendants at Nuremberg, should either by death or by imprisonment be permanently removed from civilized society. If prevention, deterrence, retribution, nay even vengeance, are ever adequate motives for punitive action, then punitive action is justified against a substantial number of Germans. But the question is: Upon what theory may that action properly be taken?

The starting point is the indictment of October 18, 1945,

charging some twenty individuals and various organizations, in four counts, with conspiracy, crimes against peace, war crimes, and crimes against humanity. Let me examine the offenses that are called in Count 3 of the indictment "war crimes," in the strict sense.

It is sometimes said that there is no international law of war crimes. But most jurists would agree that there is at least an abbreviated list of war crimes upon which the nations of the world have agreed. Thus in Articles 46 and 47 of the Hague Convention of 1907 the United States and many other countries accepted the rules that in an occupied territory of a hostile state "family honour and rights, the lives of persons, and private property, as well as religious conviction and practice, must be respected. Private property cannot be confiscated. Pillage is formally forbidden." And consistently the Supreme Court of the United States has recognized that rules of this character are part of our law. In short, there can be no doubt of the legal right of this nation, prior to the signing of a peace treaty to use a military tribunal for the purpose of trying and punishing a German if, as Count 3 charges, in occupied territory he murdered a Polish civilian, or tortured a Czech, or raped a Frenchwoman, or robbed a Belgian. Moreover, there is no doubt of the military tribunal's parallel right to try and to punish a German if he has murdered, tortured, or maltreated a prisoner of war.

In connection with war crimes of this sort there is only one question of law worth discussing here: Is it a defense to a soldier or civilian defendant that he acted under the order of a superior?

The defense of superior orders is, upon the authorities, an open question. Without going into details, it may be said that superior orders have never been recognized as a complete defense by German, Russian, or French law, and that they have not been so recognized by civilian courts in the United States or the British Commonwealth of Nations, but they tend to be taken as a complete excuse by Anglo-American military manuals. In this state of the authorities, if the International Military Tribunal in connection with a charge of a war crime refuses to recognize superior orders as a defense, it will not be making a retroactive determination or applying an ex post facto law. It will be merely settling an open question of law as every court frequently does.

The refusal to recognize the superior-order defense not only is not repugnant to the ex post facto principle, but is consonant with our ideas of justice. Basically, we cannot admit that military efficiency is the paramount consideration. And we cannot even admit that individual self-preservation is the highest value. This is not a new question. Just as it is settled that X is guilty of murder if, in order that he and Y, who are adrift on a raft, may not die of starvation, he kills their companion, Z; so a German soldier is guilty of murder if, in order that he may not be shot for disobedience and his wife tortured in a concentration camp, he shoots a Catholic priest. This is hard doctrine, but the law cannot recognize as an absolute excuse for a killing that the killer was acting under compulsion—for such a recognition not only would leave the structure of society at the mercy of criminals of sufficient ruthlessness, but also would place the cornerstone of justice on the quicksand of self-interest.

Of course, there always remains the fundamental separateness of the problem of guilt and the problem of treatment. And no one would expect a tribunal to mete out its severest penalty to a defendant who yielded to wrongdoing only out of fear of loss of his life or his family's.

Finding Legal Precedents

In addition to "war crimes," the indictment, in Count 4, charges the defendants with "crimes against humanity." This count embraces the murder, torture, and persecution of minority groups, such as Jews, inside Germany both before and after the outbreak of war. It is alleged in paragraph X of the indictment that these wrongs "constituted violations of international conventions, of internal penal laws, of the general principles of criminal law as derived from the criminal law of all civilized nations and were involved in and part of a systematic course of conduct.". . .

In paragraph X of the indictment, reference is first made to "international conventions." There is no citation of any particular international convention which in explicit words forbids a state or its inhabitants to murder its own citizens, in time either of war or of peace. I know of no such convention. And I, therefore, conclude that when the draftsman of the indictment used the phrase "international conventions" he was using the words loosely and almost analogously with the other phrase, "general principles of criminal law as derived from the criminal law of all civilized nations." He means to say that there exists, to cover the most atrocious conduct, a broad principle of universal international criminal law which is according to the law of most penal codes and public sentiment in most places, and for violations of which an offender may be tried by any new court that one or more of the world powers may create.

If that were the only basis for the trial and punishment of those who murdered or tortured German citizens, it would be a basis that would not satisfy most lawyers. It would resemble the universally condemned Nazi law of June 28, 1935, which provided: "Any person who commits an act which the law declares to be punishable or which is deserving of penalty according to the fundamental conceptions of the penal law and sound popular feeling, shall be punished." It would fly straight in the face of the most fundamental rules of criminal justice—that criminal laws shall not be ex post facto and that there shall be . . . no crime and no penalty without an antecedent law.

The feeling against a law evolved after the commission of an offense is deeply rooted. . . . If a law can be created after an offense, then power is to that extent absolute and arbitrary. To allow retroactive legislation is to disparage the principle of constitutional limitation. It is to abandon what is usually regarded as one of the essential values at the core of our democratic faith.

But, fortunately, so far as concerns murders of German minorities, the indictment was not required to invent new law. The indictment specifically mentions "internal penal laws." And these laws are enough in view of the way the question would arise in a criminal proceeding. . . .

Considering the Crime of Waging War

I turn now to Count 2 of the indictment, which charges "crimes against peace." This is the count that has attracted greatest interest. It alleges that the defendants participated "in the planning, preparation, initiation and waging of wars of aggression, which were also wars in violation of international treaties, agreements and assurances."

This charge is attacked in many quarters on the ground it rests on ex post facto law. The reply has been that in the last generation there has accumulated a mounting body of international sentiment which indicates that wars of aggression are wrong and that a killing by a person acting on behalf of an aggressor power is not an excusable homicide. . . . It is claimed that now it is unlawful to wage an aggressive war and it is criminal to aid in preparing for such a war, whether by political, military, financial, or industrial means.

One difficulty with that reply is that the body of growing custom to which reference is made is custom directed at sovereign states, not at individuals. There is no convention or treaty which places obligations explicitly upon an individual not to aid in waging an aggressive war. Thus, from the point of view of the individual, the charge of a "crime against peace" appears in one aspect like a retroactive law. At the time he acted, almost all informed jurists would have told him that individuals who engaged in aggressive war were not in the legal sense criminals.

Another difficulty is the possible bias of the Tribunal in connection with Count 2. Unlike the crimes in Counts 3 and 4, Count 2 charges a political crime. The crime which is asserted is tried not before a dispassionate neutral bench, but before the very persons alleged to be victims. There is not even one neutral sitting beside them.

And what is most serious is that there is doubt as to the sincerity of our belief that all wars of aggression are crimes. A question may be raised whether the United Nations are prepared to submit to scrutiny the attack of Russia on Poland, or on Finland or the American encouragement to the Russians to break their treaty with Japan. Every one of these actions may have been proper, but we hardly admit that they are subject to international judgment.

These considerations make the second count of the Nuremberg indictment look to be of uncertain foundation and uncertain limits. To some the count may appear as nothing more than the ancient rule that the vanquished are at the mercy of the victor. To others it may appear as the mere declaration of an always latent doctrine that the leaders of a nation are subject to outside judgment as to their motives in waging war.

Conspiracy Charges

The other feature of the Nuremberg indictment is Count 1, charging a "conspiracy." Paragraph III of the indictment alleges that the "conspiracy embraced the commission of Crimes against Peace; . . . it came to embrace the commission of War Crimes . . . and Crimes against Humanity.". . .

If the conspiracy charge in Count 1 meant no more than that those are guilty who plan a murder and with knowledge finance and equip the murderer, no one would quarrel with the count. But it would appear that Count 1 meant to establish some additional separate substantive offense of conspiracy. That is, it asserts that there is in international law a wrong which consists in acting together for an unlawful end, and that he who joins in that action is liable not only for what he planned, or participated in, or could reasonably have foreseen would happen, but is liable for what every one of his fellows did in the course of the conspiracy. Almost as broad a doctrine of conspiracy exists in municipal law.

But what is the basis for asserting so broad a substantive crime exists in the international law? Where is the treaty, the custom, the academic learning on which it is based? Is this not a type of "crime" which was first described and defined either in London or in Nuremberg sometime in the year 1945?

Aside from the fact that the notion is new, is it not fundamentally unjust? . . . After all, in a government or other large social community there exists among the top officials, civilian and military, together with their financial and industrial collaborators, a kind of over-all working arrangement which may always be looked upon, if its invidious connotation be disregarded, as a "conspiracy." That is, government implies "breathing together." And is everyone who, knowing the purposes of the party in power, participates in government or joins with officials to be held for every act of the government?

To take a case which is perhaps not so obvious, is everyone who joins a political party, even one with some illegal purposes, to be held liable to the world for the action that every member takes, even if that action is not declared in the party platform and was not known to or consented to by the person charged as a wrongdoer? . . .

Disputing the Merits of the Trial

Turning now from the legal basis of the indictment, I propose briefly to consider whether, quite apart from legal technicalities, the procedure of an international military tribunal on the Nuremberg pattern is a politically acceptable way of dealing with the offenders in the dock and those others whom we may legitimately feel should be punished.

The chief arguments usually given for this quasi-judicial trial are that it gives the culprits a chance to say anything that can be said on their behalf, that it gives both the world today and the world tomorrow a chance to see the justice of the Allied cause and the wickedness of the Nazis', and that it sets a firm foundation for a future world order wherein individuals will know that if they embark on schemes of aggression or murder or torture or persecution they will be severely dealt with by the world.

The first argument has some merit. The defendants, after hearing and seeing the evidence against them, will have an opportunity without torture and with the aid of counsel to make statements on their own behalf. For us and for them this opportunity will make the proceeding more convincing.

Yet the defendants will not have the right to make the type of presentation that at least English-speaking persons have thought the indispensable concomitant of a fair trial. No one expects that [Joachim von] Ribbentrop will be allowed to summon [Soviet Foreign Minister Vyacheslav] Molotov to disprove the charge that in invading Poland Germany started an aggressive war.* No one anticipates that the defense, if it has the evidence, will be given as long a time to present its evidence as the prosecution takes. And there is nothing more foreign to those proceedings than either the presumption that the defendants are innocent until proved guilty or the doctrine that any adverse public comment on the defendants before the verdict is prejudicial to their receiving a fair trial. The basic approach is that these men should not have a chance to go free. And that being so, they ought not to be tried in a court of law.

As to the second point, one objection is purely pragmatic. There is a reasonable doubt whether this kind of trial, despite the voluminous and accessible record it makes, persuades anyone. It brings out new evidence, but does it change men's minds? Most reporters say that the Germans are neither interested in nor persuaded by these proceedings, which they regard as partisan. They regard the proceedings not as marking a rebirth of law in Central Europe but as a political judgment on their former leaders. The same attitude may prevail in the future because of the departure from accepted legal standards.

A more profound objection to the second point is that to regard a trial as a propaganda device is to debase justice. To be sure, most trials do and should incidentally educate the public. Yet any judge knows that if he, or counsel, or the parties regard a trial primarily as a public demonstration, or even as a general inquest, then there enter considerations which would otherwise be regarded as improper. In a political inquiry and even more in the spread of propaganda,

---

* Ribbentrop and Molotov signed the German-Soviet Non-Aggression Pact at the outset of the invasion of Poland. Both countries pledged to maintain peace while dividing up Poland between them.

the appeal is likely to be to the unreflecting thought and the deep-seated emotions of the crowd untrammeled by any fixed standards. The objective is to create outside the courtroom a desired state of affairs. In a trial the appeal is to the disinterested judgment of reasonable men guided by established precepts. The objective is to make inside the courtroom a sound disposition of a pending case according to settled principles.

The argument that these trials set a firm foundation for a future world legal structure is perhaps debatable. The spectacle of individual liability for a world wrong may lead to future treaties and agreements specifying individual liability. If this were the outcome and if, for example, with respect to wars of aggression, war crimes, and use of atomic energy the nations should agree upon world rules establishing individual liability, then this would be a great gain. But it is by no means clear that this trial will further any such program.

Dangerous Precedents for International and Domestic Law

At the moment, the world is most impressed by the undeniable dignity and efficiency of the proceedings and by the horrible events recited in the testimony. But, upon reflection, the informed public may be disturbed by the repudiation of widely accepted concepts of legal justice. It may see too great a resemblance between this proceeding and others which we ourselves have condemned. If in the end there is a generally accepted view that Nuremberg was an example of high politics masquerading as law, then the trial instead of promoting may retard the coming of the day of world law.

Quite apart from the effect of the Nuremberg trial upon the particular defendants involved, there is the disturbing effect of the trial upon domestic justice here and abroad. "We but teach bloody instructions, which being taught, return to plague the inventor." Our acceptance of the notions of ex post facto law and group guilt blunt much of our criticism of Nazi law. Indeed our complaisance may mark the beginning of an age of reaction in constitutionalism in particular and of law in general. Have we forgotten that law is not power, but restraint on power?

If the Nuremberg trial of the leading Nazis should never have been undertaken, it does not follow that we should not have punished these men. It would have been consistent with our philosophy and our law to have disposed of such of the defendants as were in the ordinary sense murderers by individual, routine, undramatic, military trials. This was the course proposed in the speeches of the Archbishop of York, Viscount Cecil, Lord Wright, and others in the great debate of March 20, 1945, in the House of Lords. In such trials the evidence and the legal issues would have a stark simplicity and the lesson would be inescapable.

For those who were not chargeable with ordinary crimes only with political crimes such as planning an aggressive war, would it not have been better to proceed by an executive determination—that is, a proscription directed at certain named individuals? The form of the determination need not have been absolute on its face. It might have been a summary order reciting the offense and allowing the named persons to show cause why they should not be punished, thus giving them a chance to show any mistake of identification or gross mistake of fact. . . .

Such a disposition would avoid the inevitably misleading characteristics of the present proceedings, such as a charge presented in the form of an "indictment," the participation of celebrated civil judges and the legal formalities of rulings on evidence and on law. It is these characteristics which may make the Nuremberg trial such a potential danger to law everywhere. Moreover, if it were generally felt that we ought not to take a man's life without the form of a trial, then the executive determination could be limited to imprisonment. . . .

To be sure, such an executive determination is ex post facto. Indeed, it is a bill of attainder. To be sure it is also an exhibition of power and not of restraint. But its very merit is its naked and unassumed character. It confesses itself to be not legal justice but political. The truthful facing of the character of our action would make it more certain that the case would not become a precedent in domestic law. . . .

The Importance of Procedural Regularity

This emphasis on procedural regularity is not legalistic or, as it is sometimes now said, conceptualistic. If there is one axiom that emerges clearly from the history of constitutionalism and from the study of any bill of rights or any charter of freedom, it is that procedural safeguards are the very substance of the liberties we cherish. Not only the specific guarantees with respect to criminal trials, but the general promise of "due process of law," have always been phrased and interpreted primarily in their procedural aspect. Indeed it hardly lies in the mouth of any supporter of the Nuremberg proceedings to disparage such procedural considerations; for may it not be said that the reason that the authors of those proceedings cast them in the form of a trial was to persuade the public that the customary safeguards and liberties were preserved?

It is against this deceptive appearance, big with evil consequences for law everywhere, that as a matter of civil courage all of us, judges as well as lawyers and laymen, however silent we ordinarily are, ought to speak out. It is for their silence on such matters that we justly criticize the Germans. And it is the test of our sincere belief in justice under law never to allow it to be confused with what are merely our interest, our ingenuity, and our power.

A Just Trial

Charles E. Wyzanski Jr.

> At the time of the trial, Judge Charles E. Wyzanski Jr. of the
> U.S. District Court for Massachusetts wrote a cautionary
> article anticipating that the rights of the accused would be
> trampled and a bad precedent would be set for the future.
> After the trial, he admitted that he had been wrong. In partic-
> ular, he concluded that failing to create a new legal standard
> that insured the Nazis would be prosecuted could have
> opened the door to more arbitrary punishments. Even though
> the judge was reassured after seeing how the trial was con-
> ducted, he still believed it could have been done more fairly
> by, for example, including neutral parties in the proceed-
> ings—though he admits the Russians probably would not
> have allowed this. Wyzanski also came to appreciate some of
> the positive aspects of the trial, such as the acquisition of doc-
> umentary evidence that might have otherwise not been dis-
> covered or publicly disclosed.

The doubt which seemed to critics of the Nuremberg trial
most fundamental was whether the defendants could
properly be held to answer a charge that they had engaged
in "the crime of aggressive war." Was there any such substantive offense?

Many who replied affirmatively contended that "the crime
of aggressive war" was no different from the specific war
crimes (such as killing a captured enemy civilian) that had
been defined in the Hague Convention of 1907. That is, they
argued that waging an aggressive war was a crime that had

Excerpted from "Nuremberg in Retrospect," by Charles E. Wyzanski Jr., *The Atlantic
Monthly*, December 1946.

been outlawed by a specific treaty or treaties; and that individuals who engaged in such conduct, like individuals who engaged in the slaughter of captured civilians, were triable by any tribunal established for the occasion by a warring power, and were punishable by any penalty prescribed for the occasion by that power.

That argument seems to me unsound. It does not seem to me that an examination of the pre-war treaties, conference proposals, diplomatic correspondence, and juristic writings shows that there was a specific international covenant that individuals who waged an aggressive war were criminals in the same sense that there was a specific international covenant that individuals who killed captured civilians were criminals.

The Argument for Criminal Charges

But it is not sufficient to stop with that purely analytical approach. There remains this inquiry: Is it just to declare, after hostilities have begun, that planners of an aggressive war are criminal?

Those who believe that it is, make a twofold contention. First, they say that when these defendants planned this war both they and everyone else would have admitted that the planning of aggressive war was a violation of standards which, whether or not they had been formulated like the Hague conventions, were universally accepted by the international community in treaties and otherwise; and that no one should be surprised to see such deliberate violations stamped as criminal. Second, they say that international criminal law in its present almost primitive state is similar to early domestic criminal law, and therefore requires not only the application of enacted law and of judicial precedent, but also the retroactive declaration of new law.

At first I was shocked by those contentions. I was prepared to assent to the statement that the defendants deliberately violated standards which had been widely accepted. But I hesitated to concede that any state or group of states should have the power retroactively to affix the additional label "criminal" to conduct which, when it occurred, was commonly regarded only as a violation of accepted standards and of treaties. It seemed to me that to allow such retrospective labeling opened the door to an arbitrary selection of offenders. It struck at the roots of constitutional limitations on power and contradicted the teachings of the philosophers of liberty. Moreover, while I was prepared to assent to the proposition that some topics in international law could be, and had been, developed by judicial tribunals declaring the law retroactively, I was not aware that the particular branch of international law which dealt with individual crimes had ever been thought to be susceptible of retroactive codification by judges or by states.

Lesser Evil

On further reflection I have come to the view that the points stated in the last paragraph are not conclusive. I am now persuaded that in the formative period of international law it is just for a representative group of power retroactively to label as criminal, conduct which, when it occurred, was universally regarded as a serious violation of generally accepted international standards and treaties. To put it in a single sentence, the reasons for my change are that the failure of the international community to attach the criminal label to such universally condemned conduct would be more likely to promote arbitrary and discriminatory action by public authorities and to undermine confidence in the proposition that international agreements are made to be kept, than the failure of the international community to abide by the maxim that no act can be punished as a crime unless there was in advance of the act a specific criminal law.

It is a choice of evil. And I do not claim that my present belief can be proved to be correct. Essentially it is what the philosophers would call a value judgment based on these considerations. If the powers had not agreed upon a rational formula for indicting those who planned World War II, it is highly probable that either some state or some unauthorized individuals would arbitrarily and perhaps even ruthlessly have undertaken the punishment of capriciously chosen Nazi chieftains. If the treaties against aggression which had been negotiated prior to World War II were treated as mere statements of intention, then post-war treaties against aggression, no matter how precisely drafted, would have been regarded as imperfect obligations.

But, regardless of its provability, the scale of values which now seems to me sound puts repugnance to retroactive legislation in a less important place than repugnance to leaving unpunished serious violations of standards universally recognized by the international community and embodied in treaties and like international obligations. To guard against misapprehension, I should reiterate that the scale applies only to grave departures from standards that have been widely and formally accepted, and only when the conduct arises in the international field where and while the organs of the international community are so undeveloped and are so intermittent in their functioning that it is impractical to expect the declaration of criminality to be made in advance of the conduct.

Still Some Reservations

Thus it now seems to me to have been "just," and even probably under some civilized systems of law even "legal," to have charged the defendants with the crime of aggressive war. But, in candor, I must add that I am not satisfied that it was "legal" under American law. I can best express my reservation by example. Suppose that [Rudolf] Hess had been brought to the United States and had been here charged with, tried on, and convicted of only the crime of aggressive war by a military tribunal created by the President with or without the cooperation of other nations; and suppose that, having been sentenced to jail in the United States, he, like [Japanese general Tomoyuki] Yamashita, had sought a writ of habeas corpus from a United States judge. Would he not have had a right to be released on the ground that he was held in violation of the ex post facto clause of Article I, Section 9, of the United States Constitution? That is, does not the United States Constitution put at the very front of its scale of values a ban on retroactive criminal laws?

Before turning to the next topic, I should note parenthetically that some persons who shared my original view, that before the Nuremberg trial there was no substantive "crime of aggressive war," say that even after the Nuremberg trial they do not know what the crime is, because the victorious powers and their court have not defined the crime of which the defendants were adjudged guilty. To them the verdict implies no more than the proposition that the victors are empowered to punish the vanquished. They say that there is no definition as to when a war is "aggressive" and that there is no rule laid down for distinguishing between the organizers and the participants in such an aggressive war.

To this the answers are that the definition of "aggressive," like other legal terms, will acquire content by exemplification; and the full meaning will become clear only after sufficient cases have been brought before and adjudicated by competent tribunals. It may be difficult at some future time to determine whether a particular war is an aggressive war, but there was no difficulty in deciding that the Nazi war was an aggressive war, since it would be generally conceded that the term "aggressive war" at its least includes a war like the Nazi war, which is begun by an attack by those who do not themselves believe that they are in danger of immediate attack by others. And although it may be difficult to say how far down the line of command responsibility goes, responsibility certainly extends at least to those who, knowing there is no danger, both plan and direct the unwarranted attack.

These answers would have been more evident if it had not been for the almost absurd citations of [seventeenth-century Dutch legal scholar Hugo] Grotius and other jurists made by some supporters of the Nuremberg proceedings. These supporters often seem to argue that Grotius said (which, of course, he did not) that those who kill in the course of a war commit a legal crime unless the war is a just war; and that where a war is unjust, those who engage in it and kill their fellow men are murderers. Grotius's definitions of just and unjust wars refer primarily not to mundane but to divine justice. And he did not describe—few sensible people would describe—as murderer the common soldier required to kill his enemy in the course of an unjust war. Neither Grotius nor the powers who drafted the Nuremberg charter nor the judges or prosecutors who participated at Nuremberg have termed criminal those men who merely fought in a war not of their making. . . .

Judging the Judges

While, so far as I am aware, it was legally unobjectionable to have the defendants tried by an English judge or a French judge or an American judge, or any combination of them, can we fairly say it was unobjectionable to have the defendants tried by a Russian judge on the particular charge of aggressive war which was presented? Did not the charge refer to an aggressive attack on Poland? And (while deeply sensible of the later horrible sufferings the Russians underwent from an unprovoked attack by Germany on Russia itself) can we say that the Russians (who in advance were apprised of the proposed German attack on Poland and who participated in the division of the spoils resulting from that attack) were suitable persons to participate in judgment upon the charge that the Germans aggressively attacked Poland? This is not an issue (as it is sometimes supposed to be) whether it is just to prosecute one group of criminals (Germans) and not another (Russians). It is the simpler issue whether an apparent confederate is to sit in judgment on an alleged criminal.

While it was not legally necessary to have invited neutrals and even distinguished anti-Nazi Germans to sit in judgment at the trial, would it not have been politically wiser to have done so, since the type of issues raised by a charge of the crime of aggressive war, unlike the issues raised by a charge of strict war crimes, are so susceptible of national bias? Would not a tribunal which included some judges free of any connection with the victims of the aggressive attack have furnished a sounder precedent?

To these questions the usual, but not entirely satisfactory, answers are that the authors of the Nuremberg procedure believed that distinguished neutrals would not accept appointment, and that the Russians would not have sat with neutrals.

Two other political, rather than legal, questions remain. First, was it desirable to include this charge in the Nuremberg indictment when there were enough other charges of a more orthodox character upon which the defendants were being tried and were likely to be hanged? Second, was it better to have these defendants tried before a military court or to have them disposed of by a more summary executive procedure?

The Aggressive War Charge

If the defendants had been tried solely on the grounds that they had engaged in war crimes in the strict sense and in crimes against humanity, the practical result for the men in the dock at Nuremberg would (with the single exception of Hess) have been precisely the same as it actually turned out to be. Hess is the only defendant who was convicted of the crime of aggressive war and the crime of conspiracy but was not convicted of other crimes as well.

Moreover, if the defendants had been tried solely on the grounds that they had engaged in war crimes in the strict sense and in crimes against humanity, there would from the outset have been a far greater degree of unanimity of professional opinion in support of the Nuremberg trial.

There were, however, countervailing considerations, which could well be thought more significant. If the defendants were charged only with the strict war crimes and not with the crime of aggressive war, it would have deeply offended the public sense of justice, for the public regarded the planning of the war as the greatest of crimes. To the general public it would have seemed grossly inappropriate to punish Göring only for killing a few named individuals, and not for starting a war in which millions were killed.

Furthermore, if the powers had not included in the Nuremberg indictment a charge that the defendants had committed the crime of aggressive war, not only would they have missed the opportunity to establish the doctrine that there is a world law against aggressive war, but their very silence and timidity would have weakened the force now, and perhaps for all time, of such declarations as had heretofore been made that aggressive war was outlawed.

Judicial vs. Executive Proceeding

There remains for discussion the problem whether it would have been politically wiser to have dealt with the Nuremberg defendants by a proceeding that was not judicial but frankly executive.

Before the Nuremberg trial began, those who, like myself, originally opposed a judicial proceeding stressed the following points, among others. There was a grave danger that the trial itself could not be conducted in an orderly way. . . . There seemed no likelihood that the trial would be so arranged that the defendants would be given adequate opportunity to produce evidence and to examine and cross-examine witnesses. There was skepticism as to whether any defendant had a chance to be acquitted, particularly since it appeared that the tribunal might start with a presumption of guilt rather than a presumption of innocence. And it was feared that the tribunal would focus on the propaganda aspects of the trial and would be unduly concerned with the effect of the trial upon the public opinion of the outside world. Cumulatively, these considerations made many commentators doubtful whether the court could act as a court should act. And—though this was less important—it made commentators fear that the trial instead of persuading the Germans of today or tomorrow that our side was just, would persuade them that we were hypocrites disguising vengeance under the facade of legality.

To avoid such dangers, these critics suggested that victorious powers should frankly state that for reasons which would be announced to the world, and which would include a recital of the wrongs the defendants had perpetrated and the menace they still presented, the powers proposed to deny them further liberty and, if necessary, to take their lives. Before such announcement was put into effect, the persons named for punishment would have an adequate opportunity to present any evidence they had that they had been erroneously named or charged with wrongdoing. It was believed that a course so drastic and so plainly premised on an exceptional situation would never be thought, as a trial might be thought, suitable for incorporation in the permanent fabric of domestic systems of justice.

Now that the trial has been held, many of these forebodings are shown to have been wide of the mark. Judged as a court trial, the Nuremberg proceedings were a model of forensic fairness. Lord Justice Lawrence and his associates acted with dignity and firmness and with eyes directed only to such matters as judges ought to consider.

Moreover, the very length of the trial has shown that those who originally favored a summary proceeding had overestimated the knowledge which the Allies had in advance of the trial. A year ago they did not have the specific information necessary promptly to prepare a reliable recital of who were the chief offenders and what were their offenses. Indeed, if it had not been for the trial and the diligent efforts of the staff of able lawyers and investigators, acting promptly and in response to the necessities of legal technique, the important documents in which the defendants convicted themselves might never have been uncovered. Thus the trial gave the victorious powers the adequate record which they required for proper disposition of the defendants and simultaneously gave historians much of the data which the world will require for proper evaluation of the causes and events of World War II.

But the outstanding accomplishment of the trial which could never have been achieved by any more summary executive action, is that it has crystallized the concept that there already is inherent in the international community a machinery both for the expression of international criminal law and for its enforcement. The great powers of the world have agreed that it is in accordance with justice for a group of nations to establish on an ad hoc basis a tribunal, first, to review the state of world opinion on conduct, in order to determine whether that conduct, when it occurred, was so universally condemned as an international wrong that it can be called a "crime"; and second, to apply that determination to individuals.

No doubt such an ad hoc method is not satisfactory as a covenant made by all the powers in advance of wrongful conduct—a covenant describing such conduct, fixing the tribunal which shall try offenders and fixing the penalty which shall be imposed. But until the world is prepared to follow the more satisfactory method, it has every reason to be profoundly grateful to Mr. Justice Jackson and his associates, who, in the face of enormous practical difficulties and widespread theoretical criticisms, persisted until they demonstrated the justice of the ad hoc method adopted at Nuremberg.

The Rights of the Accused Were Protected at Nuremberg

Benjamin B. Ferencz

Those who simply wanted to see the Nazis punished for their acts during the war were not particularly concerned with the specifics of criminal procedure, but many thoughtful people were worried that the Nuremberg Trials would be a sham because the accused had such a notorious reputation that their rights would be trampled or ignored. However, Benjamin B. Ferencz, a prosecutor at Nuremberg, notes that the trial was open so that no one could accuse the major powers of wrong-doing and that any effort to railroad the defendants would have been plain to all. If anything the Allies bent over backwards to treat the Germans fairly, from allowing the defendants to choose any lawyer they wanted to providing their counsels with generous rations, salaries, and other perks. Most technical rules also favored the defendants or were adapted to ensure their rights were protected, such as providing German translations of documents. In the end, Ferencz believes results of the trial attest to the impartial way it was conducted.

Since the trial of major war criminals by the first International Military Tribunal was completed in October 1946, twelve other cases have been presented in Nuremberg against German nationals charged with the commission of

Reprinted, with the author's permission, from "Nurnberg Trial Procedure and the Rights of the Accused," by Benjamin B. Ferencz, *The Journal of Criminal Law and Criminology*, vol. 39, no. 2 (April 23, 1948). (Endnotes in the original have been omitted in this reprint.)

crimes against peace, war crimes, and crimes against humanity. Judgments have been rendered in eight cases, and the remaining four cases are in various stages of completion. These subsequent proceedings against leading [Nazis] conducting in the name of the United States have in fact been international trials. The Military Tribunals enforcing established international law were constituted in the American zone* in pursuance of legislation enacted by the four occupying powers and similar tribunals were established in the other zones of occupation. That the crimes charged in these proceedings were punishable under preexisting laws has already been the subject of detailed examination and need not be here discussed. The landmarks in international law, which have been erected in Nuremberg, rest on a foundation of legal procedure that has satisfied the traditional safeguards of Continental and American law. The details of these rights and privileges, assuring a fair and impartial trial to each accused are but little known and worthy of consideration.

The facts that members of a defeated nation are tried in tribunals of the victor creates the need for closest scrutiny of the proceedings but does not necessarily or by itself render the conduct of the trials corrupt. Such processes are as old as war itself and have been conducted by the United States since [the Revolutionary War]. Though the Nuremberg Tribunals, being international courts, are technically not bound by the laws of the United States, it is significant to note that the Supreme Court has recognized that the establishment of Military Tribunals to punish offenses against the Law of Nations is in full accord with Articles I and II of the United States Constitution. The Court pointed out that:

> An important incident to the conduct of war is the adoption of measures by the Military command not only to repel and defeat the enemy, but to seize and subject to disciplinary measures those enemies who, in their attempt to thwart or impede our military effort have violated the law of war.

---

* After its defeat, Germany was divided into zones that were independently controlled by one of the Allied powers.

In a later case, the Supreme Court stated that:

> The trial and punishment of enemy combatants who have committed violations of the law of war is thus not only a part of the conduct of war operating as a preventive measure against such violations, but is an exercise of the authority sanctioned by Congress to administer the system of military justice recognized by the law of war.

Following the many declarations made by the United Nations, which warned the Germans and held out hope and promise to the oppressed, it became the moral duty of the liberator not to forsake those pledges and to bring the criminals to trial. This became one of the very purposes of the war. Yet it is only a figure of speech to say, "the Vanquished are tried by the Victors." The individual offenders placed on trial are no more "Vanquished" than an ordinary criminal apprehended by police representing law-abiding society. The conflict that engulfed most of the world left no real neutrals whose interests were completely unaffected. . . . The proceedings of Nuremberg, though conducted by the United States were always open to the German public. Correspondents and visitors from all parts of the world attended the trials without restriction or limitation. The written daily transcripts in German and English have always been available to anyone who cared about them. Where the complete record is readily available for the scrutiny or criticism of legal scholars the danger of tyranny is destroyed. The existence of American critics proves that there can be unbiased American judges. The judges were actually selected from prominent and respected members of some of the leading courts in the United States. Under such circumstances, the fact that the tribunals are composed of American jurists does not detract from the sincerity and fairness of the trials.

Military Government enacted legislation to ensure the rights of the defendants. A committee of the Presiding Judges of the Tribunals adopted rules of procedure consistent with the laws of Military Government and these rules were revised from time to time if it appeared that any hardship or difficulty of procedure existed.

Concessions to the Defense

Every defendant has had the right under the law to be represented by counsel of his own selection, providing such counsel was qualified to conduct cases before German courts or was specifically authorized by the Tribunal. In practice this has meant that no German lawyer has ever been excluded if he was requested as counsel for a defendant. . . . If tried, many of them would be barred from legal practice but they have, through the intervention of the American authorities, even been given immunity from prosecution in their own courts in order to ensure that accused criminals will have a free choice of counsel from those Germans whom they consider best suited to defend them. Only three defendants requested American counsel. Two of these requests were promptly approved. The other, which was a request made late in the trial to have an American substituted for one of the German counsel who had previously been selected by the defendant himself, was disapproved. The Tribunal expressed doubt of the sincerity of the application when pointing out that the American was not, in fact, available. It was the opinion of the judges before whom he was to appear that the attorney had by his previous conduct defying orders of the Military Governor and by his violation of standing Military Government regulations disqualified himself. The right of a Tribunal to protect itself from abuse by unscrupulous practitioners is inherent in every court and in exercising that right in the one case, the Nuremberg judges made it clear that they did not intend to bar the defendants from the ethical employment of reputable American counsel. This same tribunal later approved American counsel for another defendant.

The solicitude shown the defendants is reflected in the privileges accorded their counsel. The highest number of prosecuting attorneys employed in Nuremberg for all trials was 75 as compared with the 191 German lawyers engaged for the defense. The United States Government provides a separate mess for the defense lawyers, where three adequate meals including American coffee are supplied. By command of the Military authorities all defense lawyers are given the largest German ration allowance, authorizing them 3900

Justice Is Never Neutral

While the initial impulse of some of the Allies was to dispense with trials and summarily execute the Nazis they considered criminals, the decision to hold trials to determine guilt was not universally viewed as a step toward justice. The Allies were immediately accused of being unable to conduct a fair trial because they could not be impartial after being victims of Nazi aggression. A.L. Goodheart, a professor at Oxford, explains, however, that the notion of impartial justice is somewhat illusory.

It has been argued that the Tribunal cannot be regarded as a court in the true sense because, as its members represent the victorious Allied Nations, they must lack that impartiality which is an essential in all judicial procedure. According to this view only a court consisting of neutrals, or, at least, containing some neutral judges, could be considered to be a proper tribunal. As no man can be a judge in his own case, so no allied tribunal can be a judge in a case in which members of the enemy government or forces are on trial. Attractive as this argument may sound in theory, it ignores the fact that it runs counter to the administration of law in every country. If it were true then no spy could be given a legal trial, because his case is always heard by judges representing the enemy country. Yet no one has ever argued that in such cases it was necessary to call on neutral judges. The prisoner has the right to demand that his judges shall be fair, but not that they shall be neutral. As Lord Writ has pointed out, the same principle is applicable to ordinary criminal law because "a burglar cannot complain that he is being tried by a jury of honest citizens."

A.L. Goodheart, "The Legality of the Nuremberg Trials," *Juridical Review,* April 1946.

calories daily, which is more than the amount received by American soldiers and almost three times the amount available to the average German. In addition, each one is gratuitously issued a very highly prized carton of American cigarettes per week, which is a privilege afforded no employees of Military Government regardless of nationality of position. American air, rail, and motor transportation is authorized and American gasoline is given to those with private vehicles for their official use. Their salaries of 3500 marks per defendant are paid by the local Government and may be as high as 7000 marks per month as contrasted with the 200 marks received monthly by the average skilled worker. All needed office space for attorneys and clerical help is provided without charge. It may be fairly stated that the assistance given the Nuremberg defendants has been greater than that available to the average impecunious defendant in America.

The law requires that the indictment state the charges plainly, concisely and with sufficient particulars to inform the defendants of the offenses charged. At least 30 days must elapse between the service of the indictment and the beginning of the trial, and this has generally been exceeded. The time thus allowed for the defendant to prepare his case is greater than that required by German or American criminal or military law, and every defendant has received with the indictment German copies of all pertinent laws, rules, and regulations.

Every defendant has the right to be present throughout the trial, which is conducted in German and English simultaneously by the use of interpreters and earphones. A sound recording of the verbal proceedings is made and used to check the accuracy of the translations and stenographic transcripts. These are promptly available to defense attorneys for use or correction.

Each defendant has the right through his counsel to present evidence in support of his defense, and may testify for himself, which is a right denied by continental law. All personnel, facilities and supplies for translation, photostating and mimeographing are available on equal terms to Defense and Prosecution.

Technical Rules

The Military Government Ordinance providing for the establishment of Military Tribunals specifically provides that the Tribunals shall not be bound by technical rules but shall admit any evidence which they deem to contain information of probative value relating to the charges. Affidavits, interrogations, letters, diaries, and other statements may therefore be admitted. The opposing party is given the opportunity to question the authenticity or probative value of all such evidence. Objection has been raised that this is broader than the rules applied in courts of the United States and therefore somehow deprives the defendants of a fair trial of the due process of law required in American courts by the 5th Amendment. This question was brought before the Supreme Court of the United States when the Japanese General Yamashita was convicted by a military commission where similar rules of evidence prevailed. The Court held that Congress had authorized the establishment of such rules by the Military Commander and they were subject only to review of the Military authorities. No case has been held to be unfair even though such rules have prevailed before British and American Military Commissions in the Pacific, Mediterranean, and European Theaters and were in fact provided for in the Charter of the International Military Tribunal which was accepted and ratified by 23 countries and affirmed by the General Assembly of the United Nations. Due process of law does not require any particular type of tribunal so long as the proceedings afford the accused an impartial hearing and adequate safeguards for the protection of his individual rights. Exclusionary rules of evidence arose in ancient Anglo-American common law to prevent erroneous conclusions that might be drawn by a lay jury receiving insubstantial proof. Where only judges skilled in the law weigh the evidence, no such danger exists. The numerous exceptions to the American "hearsay rule" admit far more evidence than they exclude and no rule exists in German law to exclude hearsay proof. The captured official German documents, which constitute the bulk of the prosecution's case, have considerable probative value and to exclude such evidence that in many respects is more reliable than the report years later of a prejudiced or emotional eyewitness would be the height of folly. The weight given to particular pieces of evidence varies, of course, with the nature of the proof, and the failure to impose rigid technical rules on expert triers of fact and law in no way damages the substantial rights of the defense. By ruling of the Tribunals no document or exhibit may be offered against a defendant unless a German copy has been given to his counsel at least 24 hours in advance. Usually the documents are furnished to the defense several days or even weeks in advance which is a privilege not accorded in German or American criminal or military courts. The accused may apply to the Tribunal for the procurement of documents on their behalf and these are brought to Nuremberg by the occupation authorities.

Where affidavits are admitted the opposing side may call the witnesses for cross-examination or if it is physically impossible for the witness to appear, cross-interrogatories or cross-affidavits may be submitted. The use of affidavits by the Prosecution has in fact been negligible as compared to that of the Defense and their admissibility has been an advantage to the defendants.

Each defendant, through his personal counsel, may cross-examine any witness called by the Prosecution and at his request the American authorities will transport to Nuremberg, feed, house and arrange payment for all witnesses for the defense. Prosecution witnesses share the same facilities, and once a witness is brought to Nuremberg, he may be interrogated freely by the side at whose request he was produced, or by the opposing side at whose request he was produced, or by the opposing side with the requesting party having the right to be present. There is absolutely no limitation on the defense concerning dealings with potential witnesses outside of Nuremberg and all friends and relatives of the accused are free to act on his behalf. The only potential witnesses held in confinement by the Prosecution are those who cannot be released because they are subject to automatic arrest by the German authorities or are themselves awaiting trial. The methods employed in the interrogations have always been subject to scrutiny when the witness took the stand. There has never been a finding that force was ever employed by the Prosecution to obtain information from a witness or the accused.

Motions of either side are filed in both languages, with the adverse party having 72 hours in which to reply. At the conclusion of the trial, every defendant is allowed to address the Tribunal, which is a right denied by Anglo-American law.

Any defendant may call a joint session of the Military Tribunals to review any inconsistent ruling on legal questions which affect him, or any decision or judgment which is inconsistent with a prior ruling of another of the Military Tribunals.

The full opportunity given the accused to present their defense explains largely the duration of the trials. Invariably the defense takes much longer than the prosecution and in one case the defense lasted 72 days as compared with the prosecution's case of two days.

The Results Show Fairness

The sentences actually imposed in the Nuremberg trials defeat the contention that they have been an instrument of vengeance. Germans, as well as Americans, have condemned the leniency increasingly shown by the Courts in these trials of major offenders. Of the 108 persons sentenced in the first seven cases, 20 were acquitted, 25 were sentenced to death, and in one of the most recent cases 5 high-ranking SS officers, who were convicted of membership in a criminal organization with knowledge of its criminal activities, were promptly released. The Tribunals have never exercised their power to deprive defendants of civil rights or to impose a fine or forfeiture of property, although it is almost a certainty that any defendant convicted by a German court would have been subjected to some or all of these penalties in addition to confinement.

Upon the completion of every trial the record of the case is sent to the Military Governor for review. He has power to mitigate, reduce, or otherwise alter the sentence imposed, but may not increase its severity. No death sentence may be carried into execution unless and until confirmed in writing by the Military Governor. The defendants have been given the privilege of sending petitions for review to the US Supreme Court and other high governmental offices. The Court has twice refused to review the Nuremberg cases, yet as of this writing no death sentence has been carried out though most of them were pronounced over six months ago.

It should be apparent to every unbiased critic that the good name of the United States has been upheld in Nuremberg by administering justice according to law and that those accused of war crimes "have been given the kind of a trial which they, in the days of their pomp and power, never gave to any man."

Chapter 4

The Verdicts and Conclusions

Chapter Preface

The Nuremberg Trial could have satisfied most people, and certainly the public in the Allied nations, if it had been conducted solely for the purpose of meting out justice for the crimes committed during World War II. The prosecutors, however, had even loftier goals. They wanted to make an example of the Germans that would discourage people from making war in the future, or at least prevent them from committing the types of atrocities against civilians and combatants that were routine under the Nazis.

In hindsight, these objectives appear utopian. Aggressors never expect to lose the wars they start, so they should not be expected to worry much about the consequences of their actions. Even if they were to behave humanely—if such a thing is possible during a war—losers of a future war could hardly expect to be treated better by the victors if they followed the "rules of war."

The commission of war crimes is not restricted to the "bad guys," either. Nations that may go to war in self-defense or to defend democracy may also engage in actions that warrant investigation and sometimes punishment. The hope is that democratic nations will be much less likely to commit crimes and, if they do, that they will also be willing to expose them and punish the people responsible. This happened in the case of the My Lai massacre, when American soldiers murdered more than three hundred civilians during the Vietnam War. It took more than a year for the incident to be disclosed, but when it was, a trial was held and the commander was convicted of murder.

Looking at the many wars that have followed World War II and the atrocities committed in places like Rwanda, Cambodia, and the Balkans, it is clear that the goals of Nuremberg were not achieved, but they should not be evaluated simply by today's standards. It is important to consider the prosecutors' ambition in the context of the end of the most destructive conflict in history. This was a time of renewed optimism for a better world; the United Nations was being created to settle disputes by peaceful means, and there was hope that the memory of the war's destructiveness would make international cooperation, rather than competition, the norm.

The Prosecution's Closing Speech

Robert H. Jackson

> The Nuremberg Trial was so long and complex, the attorneys
> from the four powers divided up the work. The chief counsel
> of the United States was given the task of summarizing the
> evidence that the defendants had been part of a conspiracy to
> commit war crimes. This was perhaps the most difficult
> charge to prove because it required evidence that all of the
> defendants knew of the crimes and made decisions that
> directly or indirectly resulted in their commission. One rea-
> son this charge was necessary was to prevent high German
> officials from escaping responsibility by claiming they did
> not personally commit all the crimes. The defendants would
> have liked, for example, to have only the men who pulled the
> triggers be tried for murder while those who ordered the
> killings be immune. Jackson also addressed the larger issue of
> German claims that the Nazis had acted out of self-defense.
> Though much of the evidence was convincing, the judges
> ultimately distinguished between the defendants who were
> more directly involved in conspiratorial actions and those
> who were not. Consequently, only eight of the twenty-two
> were found guilty on the conspiracy charge.

It is common to think of our own time as standing at the
apex of civilization, from which the deficiencies of pre-
ceding ages may patronizingly be viewed in the light of
what is assumed to be "progress." The reality is that in the

Excerpted from Robert H. Jackson's summary on the 187th day (July 26, 1946) of the
Nuremberg Trials, vol. 19 of the *Proceedings* (Nuremberg: International Military Tribunal,
1947).

long perspective of history the present century will not hold
an admirable position, unless its second half is to redeem its
first. These two-score years in the twentieth century will be
recorded in the book of years as one of the most bloody in
all annals. Two World Wars have left a legacy of dead which
number more than all the armies engaged in any way that
made ancient or medieval history. No half-century ever witnessed slaughter on such a scale, such cruelties and inhu-
manities, such wholesale deportations of peoples into slav-
ery, such annihilations of minorities. . . . These deeds are the
overshadowing historical facts by which generations to come
will remember this decade. If we cannot eliminate the causes
and prevent the repetition of these barbaric events, it is not
an irresponsible prophecy to say that this twentieth century
may yet succeed in bringing the doom of civilization. . . .

Germany has unconditionally surrendered, but no peace
treaty has been signed or agreed upon. The Allies are still
technically in a state of war with Germany, although the enemy's political and military institutions have collapsed. As
a military tribunal, this Tribunal is a continuation of the war
effort of the Allied nations. As an International Tribunal, it
is not bound by the procedural and substantive refinements
of our respective judicial or constitutional systems, nor will
its rulings introduce precedents into any country's internal
system of civil justice. As an International Military Tribunal,
it rises above the provincial and transient and seeks guid-
ance not only from international law but also from the basic
principles of jurisprudence which are assumptions of civilization and which long have found embodiment in the
codes of all nations.

Of one thing we may be sure. The future will never have
to ask, with misgiving, what could the Nazis have said in
their favor. History will know that whatever could be said,
they were allowed to say. They have been given the kind of
a Trial which they, in the days of their pomp and power,
never gave to any man. . . .

We have not previously and we need not now discuss the
merits of all their obscure and tortuous philosophy. We are

not trying them for the possession of obnoxious ideas. It is their right, if they choose, to renounce the Hebraic heritage in the civilization of which Germany was once a part. Nor is it our affair that they repudiated the Hellenic influence as well. The intellectual bankruptcy and moral perversion of the Nazi regime might have been no concern of international law had it not been utilized to goosestep the Herrenvolk across international frontiers. It is not their thoughts, it is their overt acts which we charge to be crimes. Their creed and teachings are important only as evidence of motive, purpose, knowledge, and intent. . . .

The Crimes of the Nazi Regime

The strength of the case against these defendants under the conspiracy Count, which it is the duty of the United States to argue, is in its simplicity. It involves but three ultimate inquiries: First, have the acts defined by the Charter as crimes been committed; second, were they committed pursuant to a Common Plan or Conspiracy; third, are these defendants among those who are criminally responsible?

The charge requires examination of a criminal policy, not of a multitude of isolated, unplanned, or disputed crimes. The substantive crimes upon which we rely, either as goals of a common plan or as means for its accomplishment, are admitted. The pillars which uphold the conspiracy charge may be found in five groups of overt acts, whose character and magnitude are important considerations in appraising the proof of conspiracy.

1. The Seizure of Power and Subjugation of Germany to a Police State.

The Nazi Party seized control of the German State in 1933. "Seizure of power" is a characterization used by defendants and defense witnesses, and so apt that it has passed into both history and everyday speech.

The Nazi junta in the early days lived in constant fear of overthrow. [Hermann] Göring, in 1934, pointed out that its enemies were legion and said:

"Therefore, the concentration camps have been created,

where we have first confined thousands of Communists and social democrat functionaries."

In 1933 Göring forecast the whole program of purposeful cruelty and oppression when he publicly announced: "Whoever in the future raises a hand against a representative of the National Socialist movement or of the State must know that he will lose his life in a very short while."

New political crimes were created to this end. It was made a treason, punishable with death, to organize or support a political party other than the Nazi Party. Circulating a false or exaggerated statement, or one which would harm the State or even the Party, was made a crime. Laws were enacted of such ambiguity that they could be used to punish almost any innocent act. It was, for example, made a crime to provoke "any act contrary to the public welfare.". . . .

The Gestapo and the SD were instrumentalities of an espionage system which penetrated public and private life. Göring controlled a personal wire-tapping unit. All privacy of communication was abolished. Party Blockleiter [neighborhood leaders] appointed over every 50 householders spied continuously on all within their ken.

Upon the strength of this spying individuals were dragged off to "protective custody" and to concentration camps without legal proceedings of any kind and without statement of any reason therefor. The partisan Political Police were exempted from effective legal responsibility for their acts.

With all administrative offices in Nazi control and with the Reichstag [German parliament] reduced to impotence, the judiciary remained the last obstacle to this reign of terror. But its independence was soon overcome and it was reorganized to dispense a venal justice. Judges were ousted for political or racial reasons and were spied upon and put under pressure to join the Nazi Party. After the Supreme Court had acquitted three of the four men whom the Nazis accused of setting the Reichstag fire, its jurisdiction over treason cases was transferred to a newly established "People's Court" consisting of two judges and five Party officials. The German film of this "People's Court" in operation, which we showed in this chamber, revealed its presiding judge pouring partisan abuse on speechless defendants. Special courts were created to try political crimes, only Party members were appointed judges, and "judges' letters" instructed the puppet judges as to the "general lines" they must follow.

The result was the removal of all peaceable means either to resist or to change the Government. Having sneaked through the portals of power, the Nazis slammed the gate in the face of all others who might also aspire to enter. Since the law was what the Nazis said it was, every form of opposition was rooted out and every dissenting voice throttled. Germany was in the clutch of a police state, which used the fear of the concentration camp as a means to enforce non-resistance. The Party was the State, the State was the Party, and terror by day and death by night were the policy of both.

2. The Preparation and Waging of Wars of Aggression.

From the moment the Nazis seized power, they set about feverish but stealthy efforts, in defiance of the Versailles Treaty, to arm for war. In 1933 they found no air force. By 1939 they had 21 squadrons, consisting of 240 echelons or about 2,400 first-line planes, together with trainers and transports. In 1933 they found an army of 3 infantry and 3 cavalry divisions. By 1939 they had raised and equipped an army of 51 divisions, 4 of which were fully motorized and 4 of which were Panzer divisions. In 1933 they found a navy of 1 cruiser and 6 light cruisers. By 1939 they had built a navy of 4 battleships, 1 aircraft carrier, 6 cruisers, 22 destroyers, and 54 submarines. They had also built up in that period an armament industry as efficient as that of any country in the world.

These new weapons were put to use, commencing in September 1939, in a series of undeclared wars against nations with which Germany had arbitration and nonaggression treaties, and in violation of repeated assurances. On 9/1/1939, this rearmed Germany attacked Poland. The following April witnessed the invasion and occupation of Denmark and Norway, and May saw the overrunning of Belgium, the Netherlands, and Luxembourg. Another spring saw Yugoslavia and Greece under attack, and in June 1941 came the invasion of Soviet Russia. Then Japan, which Germany had embraced as a partner, struck without warning at Pearl Harbor in December 1941 and 4 days later Germany declared war on the United States.

We need not trouble ourselves about the many abstract difficulties that can be conjured up about what constitutes aggression in doubtful cases. I shall show you, in discussing the conspiracy, that by any test ever put forward by any responsible authority, by all the canons of plain common sense, these were unlawful wars of aggression in breach of treaties and in violation of assurances.

3. Warfare in Disregard of International Law.

It is unnecessary to labor this point on the facts. Göring asserts that the Rules of Land Warfare were obsolete, that no nation could fight a total war within their limits. He testified that the Nazis would have denounced the conventions to which Germany was a party, but that General [Alfred] Jodl wanted captured German soldiers to continue to benefit from their observance by the Allies.

It was, however, against the Soviet people and Soviet prisoners that Teutonic fury knew no bounds, in spite of a warning by Admiral Canaris that the treatment was in violation of international law.

We need not, therefore, for the purposes of the conspiracy Count, recite the revolting details of starving, beating, murdering, freezing, and mass extermination admittedly used against the Eastern soldiery. Also, we may take as established or admitted that the lawless conduct such as shooting British and American airmen, mistreatment of Western prisoners of war, forcing French prisoners of war into German war work, and other deliberate violations of the Hague and Geneva Conventions, did occur, and in obedience to highest levels of authority.

4. Enslavement and Plunder of Populations in Occupied Countries.

The Defendant [Fritz] Sauckel, Plenipotentiary General for the Utilization of Labor, is authority for the statement that "out of 5,000,000 foreign workers who arrived in Germany, not even 200,000 came voluntarily." It was officially reported to Defendant Rosenberg that in his territory "recruiting methods were used which probably have their origin in the blackest period of the slave trade." Sauckel himself reported that male and female agents went hunting for men, got them drunk, and "shanghaied" them to Germany. These captives were shipped in trains without heat, food, or sanitary facilities. The dead were thrown out at stations, and the newborn were thrown out the windows of moving trains.

Sauckel ordered that "all the men must be fed, sheltered, and treated in such a way as to exploit them to the highest possible extent at the lowest conceivable degree of expenditure." About two million of these were employed directly in the manufacture of armaments and munitions. The director of the Krupp locomotive factory in Essen complained to the company that Russian forced laborers were so underfed that they were too weakened to do their work, and the Krupp doctor confirmed their pitiable condition. Soviet workers were put in camps under Gestapo guards, who were allowed to punish disobedience by confinement in a concentration camp or by hanging on the spot.

Populations of occupied countries were otherwise exploited and oppressed unmercifully. Terror was the order of the day. Civilians were arrested without charges, committed without counsel, executed without hearing. Villages were destroyed, the male inhabitants shot or sent to concentration camps, the women sent to forced labor, and the children scattered abroad. The extent of the slaughter in Poland alone was indicated by [Hans] Frank, who reported, and I quote: "If I wanted to have a poster put up for every seven Poles who were shot, the forests of Poland would not suffice for producing the paper for such posters.". . .

5. Persecution and Extermination of Jews and Christians.
The Nazi movement will be of evil memory in history because of its persecution of the Jews, the most far-flung and terrible racial persecution of all time. Although the Nazi Party neither invented nor monopolized anti-Semitism, its

leaders from the very beginning embraced it, incited it, and exploited it. They used it as "the psychological spark that ignites the mob." After the seizure of power it became an official state policy. The persecution began in a series of discriminatory laws eliminating the Jews from the civil service, the professions, and economic life. As it became more intense it included segregation of Jews in ghettos, and exile. Riots were organized by Party leaders to loot Jewish business places and to burn synagogues. Jewish property was confiscated and a collective fine of a billion marks was imposed upon German Jewry. The program progressed in fury and irresponsibility to the "final solution." This consisted of sending all Jews who were fit to work to concentration camps as slave laborers, and all who were not fit, which included children under 12 and people over 50, as well as any others judged unfit by an SS doctor, to concentration camps for extermination.

Adolf Eichmann, the sinister figure who had charge of the extermination program, has estimated that the anti-Jewish activities resulted in the killing of 6 million Jews. Of these, 4 million were killed in extermination institutions, and 2 million were killed by Einsatzgruppen, mobile units of the Security Police and SD which pursued Jews in the ghettos and in their homes and slaughtered them by gas wagons, by mass shooting in antitank ditches and by every device which Nazi ingenuity could conceive. So thorough and uncompromising was this program that the Jews of Europe as a race no longer exist, thus fulfilling the diabolic "prophecy" of Adolf Hitler at the beginning of the war.

Of course, any such program must reckon with the opposition of the Christian Church. This was recognized from the very beginning. Defendant [Martin] Bormann wrote . . . in 1941 that "National Socialism and Christian concepts are irreconcilable," and that the people must be separated from the churches and the influence of the churches totally removed. Defendant [Alfred] Rosenberg even wrote dreary treatises advocating a new and weird Nazi religion.

The Gestapo appointed "Church specialists" who were instructed that the ultimate aim was "destruction of the confessional churches." The record is full of specific instances of the persecution of clergymen, the confiscation of Church property, interference with religious publications, disruption of religious education and suppression of religious organizations.

The chief instrumentality for persecution and extermination was the concentration camp, sired by the Defendant Göring and nurtured under the over-all authority of Defendants [Wilhelm] Frick and [Dr. Ernst] Kaltenbrunner. . . .

The Tribunal must be satiated with ghastly verbal and pictorial portrayals. From your records it is clear that the concentration camps were the first and worst weapon of Nazi oppression used by the National Socialist State, and that they were the primary means utilized for the persecution of the Christian Church and the extermination of the Jewish race. This has been admitted to you by some of the defendants from the witness stand. In the words of Defendant Frank: "A thousand years will pass and this guilt of Germany will still not be erased.". . .

Preparing for War

Immediately after the seizure of power the Nazis went to work to implement [their] aggressive intentions by preparing for war. They first enlisted German industrialists in a secret rearmament program. Twenty days after the seizure of power [Dr. Hjalmar] Schacht was host to Hitler, Göring, and some 20 leading industrialists. Among them were Krupp von Bohlen of the great Krupp armament works and representatives of I.G. Farben and other Ruhr heavy industries. Hitler and Göring explained their program to the industrialists, who became so enthusiastic that they set about to raise 3 million Reichsmark to strengthen and confirm the Nazi Party in power. Two months later Krupp was working to bring a reorganized association of German industry into agreement with the political aims of the Nazi Government. Krupp later boasted of the success in keeping the German war industries secretly alive and in readiness despite the disarmament clauses of the Versailles Treaty [which ended

WWI and called for German disarmament], and recalled the industrialists' enthusiastic acceptance of "the great intentions of the Fuhrer in the rearmament period of 1933-39."

Some 2 months after Schacht had sponsored his first meeting to gain the support of the industrialists, the Nazis moved to harness industrial labor to their aggressive plans. In April 1933 Hitler ordered Dr. [Robert] Ley "to take over the trade unions," numbering some six million members. By Party directive Ley seized the unions, their property and their funds. Union leaders, taken into "protective custody" by the SS and SA, were put into concentration camps. The free labor unions were then replaced by a Nazi organization known as the German Labor Front, with Dr. Ley at its head. It was expanded until it controlled over 23 million members. Collective bargaining was eliminated, the voice of labor could no longer be heard as to working conditions and the labor contract was prescribed by "trustees of labor" appointed by Hitler. The war purpose of this labor program was clearly acknowledged by Robert Ley 5 days after war broke out, when he declared in a speech that: "We National Socialists have monopolized all resources and all our energies during the past 7 years so as to be able to be equipped for the supreme effort of battle.". . . .

As early as 11/5/1937 the plan to attack had begun to take definiteness as to time and victim. In a meeting which included the Defendants [Admiral Erich] Raeder, Göring, and [Baron Konstantin] von Neurath, Hitler stated the cynical objective: "The question for Germany is where the greatest possible conquest could be made at the lowest possible cost." He discussed various plans for the invasion of Austria and Czechoslovakia, indicating clearly that he was thinking of these territories not as ends in themselves, but as means for further conquest. He pointed out that considerable military and political assistance could be afforded by possession of these lands and discussed the possibility of constituting from them new armies up to a strength of about 12 divisions. The aim he stated boldly and baldly as the acquisition of additional living space in Europe, and recognized that "the German question can be solved only by way of force."

Six months later, emboldened by the bloodless Austrian conquest, Hitler, in a secret directive to [Field Marshal Wilhelm] Keitel, stated his "unalterable decision to smash Czechoslovakia by military action in the near future."

On the same day, Jodl noted in his diary that the Fuhrer had stated his final decision to destroy Czechoslovakia soon and had initiated military preparations all along the line. By April the plan had been perfected to attack Czechoslovakia "with lightning swift action as the result of an incident.". . .

This Tribunal knows what categorical assurances were given to an alarmed world after the Anschluss, after Munich, after the occupation of Bohemia and Moravia, that German ambitions were realized and that Hitler had "no further territorial demands to make in Europe." The record of this Trial shows that those promises were calculated deceptions and that those high in the bloody brotherhood of Nazidom knew it.

As early as 4/15/1938 Göring pointed out to [Italian dictator Benito] Mussolini and [Italian foreign minister Count Galeazzo] Ciano that the possession of those territories would make possible an attack on Poland. . . .

While a credulous world slumbered, snugly blanketed with perfidious assurances of peaceful intentions, the Nazis prepared not as before for a war but now for the war. The Defendants Göring, Keitel, Raeder, Frick, and [Walther] Funk, with others, met as the Reich Defense Council in June of 1939. The minutes, authenticated by Göring, are revealing evidences of the way in which each step of Nazi planning dovetailed with every other. These five key defendants, 3 months before the first Panzer unit had knifed into Poland, were laying plans for "employment of the population in wartime," and had gone so far as to classify industry for priority in labor supply after "5 million servicemen had been called up.". . .

It is the minutes of this significant conclave of many key defendants which disclose how the plan to start the war was coupled with the plan to wage the war through the use of illegal sources of labor to maintain production. . . .

Slave Labor

Here also comes to the surface the link between war labor and concentration camps, a manpower source that was increasingly used and with increasing cruelty. An agreement between [Gestapo chief Heinrich] Himmler and the Minister of Justice Thierack in 1942 provided for "the delivery of antisocial elements from the execution of their sentence to the Reichsfuhrer SS to be worked to death." An SS directive provided that bedridden prisoners be drafted for work to be performed in bed. The Gestapo ordered 46,000 Jews arrested to increase the "recruitment of manpower into the concentration camps." One hundred thousand Jews were brought from Hungary to augment the camps' manpower. On the initiative of the Defendant [Admiral Karl] Donitz, concentration camp labor was used in the construction of submarines. Concentration camps were thus geared into war production on the one hand, and into the administration of justice and the political aims of the Nazis on the other.

The use of prisoner-of-war labor as then planned in that meeting also grew with German needs. At a time when every German soldier was needed at the front and forces were not available at home, Russian prisoners of war were forced to man antiaircraft guns against Allied planes. Field Marshal [Erhard] Milch reflected the Nazi merriment at this flagrant violation of international law, saying: ". . . this is an amusing thing, that the Russians must work the guns.". . .

Other crimes in the conduct of warfare were planned with equal thoroughness as a means of insuring victory of German arms. . . . A typical Keitel order, demanding the use of the "most brutal means," provided that: ". . . It is the duty of the troops to use all means without restriction, even against women and children, so long as it insures success."

The German naval forces were no more immune from the infection than the land forces. Raeder ordered violations of the accepted rules of warfare wherever necessary to gain strategic successes. Donitz urged his submarine crews not to rescue survivors of torpedoed enemy ships in order to cripple merchant shipping of the Allied Nations by decimating their crews.

Thus, the war crimes against Allied forces and the crimes against humanity committed in occupied territories are incontestably part of the program for making the war because, in the German calculations, they were indispensable to its hope of success. . . .

The same war purpose was dominant in the persecution of the Jews. In the beginning, fanaticism and political opportunism played a principal part, for anti-Semitism and its allied scapegoat, mythology, was a vehicle on which the Nazis rode to power. It was for this reason that the filthy [Julius] Streicher and the blasphemous Rosenberg were welcomed at Party rallies and made leaders and officials of the State or Party. But the Nazis soon regarded the Jews as foremost among the opposition to the police state with which they planned to put forward their plans of military aggression. Fear of their pacifism and their opposition to strident nationalism was given as the reason that the Jews had to be driven from the political and economic life of Germany. Accordingly, they were transported like cattle to the concentration camps, where they were utilized as a source of forced labor for war purposes.

At a meeting held on 11/12/1938, 2 days after the violent anti-Jewish pogroms instigated by [Paul Joseph] Goebbels and carried out by the Party Leadership Corps and the SA, the program for the elimination of Jews from the German economy was mapped out by Göring, Funk, [Reinhard] Heydrich, Goebbels, and the other top Nazis. The measures adopted included confinement of the Jews in ghettos, cutting off their food supply, "Aryanizing" their shops, and restricting their freedom of movement. Here another purpose behind the Jewish persecutions crept in, for it was the wholesale confiscation of their property which helped finance German rearmament. Although Schacht's plan to have foreign money ransom the entire race within Germany was not adopted, the Jews were stripped to the point where Göring was able to advise the Reich Defense Council that the critical situation of the Reich exchequer, due to rearmament, had been relieved "through the billion Reichsmark fine imposed on Jewry, and through profits accrued to the Reich in the Aryanization of Jewish enterprises."

A glance over the dock will show that, despite quarrels among themselves, each defendant played a part which fitted in with every other, and that all advanced the common plan. It contradicts experience that men of such diverse backgrounds and talents should so forward each other's aims by coincidence. . . .

Defense Fallacies

The defendants contend, however, that there could be no conspiracy involving aggressive war because: (1) None of the Nazis wanted war; (2) rearmament was only intended to provide the strength to make Germany's voice heard in the family of nations and (3) the wars were not in fact aggressive wars but were defensive against a "Bolshevik menace.". . .

At the outset this argument of self-defense falls because it completely ignores this damning combination of facts clearly established in the record: First, the enormous and rapid German preparations for war; second, the repeatedly avowed intentions of the German leaders to attack, which I have previously cited; and third, the fact that a series of wars occurred in which German forces struck the first blows, without warning, across the borders of other nations. Even if it could be shown—which it cannot—that the Russian war was really defensive, such is demonstrably not the case with those wars which preceded it. It may also be pointed out that even those who would have you believe that Germany was menaced by Communism also compete with each other in describing their opposition to the disastrous Russian venture. Is it reasonable that they would have opposed that war if it were undertaken in good-faith self-defense? . . .

In all the documents which disclose the planning and rationalization of these attacks, not one sentence has been or can be cited to show a good-faith fear of attack. . . .

In opening this case I ventured to predict that there would

be no serious denial that the crimes charged were committed, and that the issue would concern the responsibility of particular defendants. The defendants have fulfilled that prophecy. Generally, they do not deny that these things happened, but it is contended that they "just happened," and that they were not the result of a common plan or conspiracy.

One of the chief reasons the defendants say there was no conspiracy is the argument that conspiracy was impossible with a dictator. The argument runs that they all had to obey Hitler's orders, which had the force of law in the German State, and hence obedience could not be made the basis of an original charge. In this way it is explained that while there have been wholesale killings, there have been no murderers.

This argument is an effort to evade Article 8 of the Charter, which provides that the order of the Government or of a superior shall not free a defendant from responsibility but can only be considered in mitigation. This provision of the Charter corresponds with the justice and with the realities of the situation, as indicated in Defendant [Albert] Speer's description of what he considered to be the common responsibility of the leaders of the German nation: ". . . with reference to utterly decisive matters, there is total responsibility. There must be total responsibility insofar as a person is one of the leaders, because who else could assume responsibility for the development of events, if not the immediate associates who work with and around the head of the State?"

Again he told the Tribunal: ". . . it is impossible after the catastrophe to evade this total responsibility. If the war had been won, the leaders would also have assumed total responsibility.". . .

The measure of the criminality of the plan and therefore of the guilt of each participant is, of course, the sum total of crimes committed by all in executing the plan. But the gist of the offense is participation in the formulation or execution of the plan. These are rules which every society has found necessary in order to reach men, like these defendants, who never get blood on their own hands but who lay plans that result in the shedding of blood. All over Germany today, in every zone of occupation, little men who carried out these criminal policies under orders are being convicted and punished. It would present a vast and unforgivable caricature of justice if the men who planned these policies and directed these little men should escape all penalty. These men in this dock, on the face of this record, were not strangers to this program of crime, nor was their connection with it remote or obscure. We find them in the very heart of it. The positions they held show that we have chosen defendants of self evident responsibility. They are the very top surviving authorities in their respective fields and in the Nazi State. No one lives who, at least until the very last moments of the war, outranked Göring in position, power, and influence. No soldier stood above Keitel and Jodl, and no sailor above Raeder and Donitz. Who can be responsible for the diplomacy of duplicity if not the Foreign Ministers, Von Neurath and [Joachim von] Ribbentrop, and the diplomatic handy man [Franz] von Papen? Who should be answerable for the oppressive administration of occupied countries if Gauleiters, protectors, governors and Kommissars such as Frank, [Dr. Arthur] Seyss-Inquart, Frick, [Baldur] von Schirach, Von Neurath, and Rosenberg are not? Where shall we look for those who mobilized the economy for total war if we overlook Schacht and Speer and Funk? Who was the master of the great slaving enterprise if it was not Sauckel? Where shall we find the hand that ran the concentration camps if it was not the hand of Kaltenbrunner? And who whipped up the hates and fears of the public, and manipulated the Party organizations to incite these crimes, if not [Rudolf] Hess, Von Schirach, [Hans] Fritzsche, Bormann, and the unspeakable Julius Streicher? The list of defendants is made up of men who played indispensable and reciprocal parts in this tragedy. . . .

To escape the implications of their positions and the inference of guilt from their activities, the defendants are almost unanimous in one defense. The refrain is heard time and again: These men were without authority, without knowledge, without influence, without importance. Funk summed up the general self-abasement of the dock in his plaintive lament that: "I always, so to speak, came up to the door, but I was not permitted to enter."

In the testimony of each defendant, at some point there was reached the familiar blank wall: Nobody knew anything about what was going on. Time after time we have heard the chorus from the dock: "I only heard about these things here for the first time."

These men saw no evil, spoke none, and none was uttered in their presence. This claim might sound very plausible if made by one defendant. But when we put all their stories together, the impression which emerges of the Third Reich, which was to last a thousand years, is ludicrous. If we combine only the stories of the front bench, this is the ridiculous composite picture of Hitler's Government that emerges. It was composed of:

A Number 2 man who knew nothing of the excesses of the Gestapo which he created, and never suspected the Jewish extermination program although he was the signer of over a score of decrees which instituted the persecutions of that race;

A Number 3 man who was merely an innocent middleman transmitting Hitler's orders without even reading them, like a postman or delivery boy;

A foreign minister who knew little of foreign affairs and nothing of foreign policy;

A field marshal who issued orders to the Armed Forces but had no idea of the results they would have in practice;

A security chief who was of the impression that the policing functions of his Gestapo and SD were somewhat on the order of directing traffic;

A Party philosopher who was interested in historical research and had no idea of the violence which his philosophy was inciting in the twentieth century;

A governor general of Poland who reigned but did not rule;

A Gauleiter of Franconia whose occupation was to pour forth filthy writings about the Jews, but who had no idea that anybody would read them;

A minister of interior who knew not even what went on in the interior of his own office, much less the interior of his own department, and nothing at all about the interior of Germany;

A Reichsbank president who was totally ignorant of what went in and out of the vaults of his bank;

And a plenipotentiary for the war economy who secretly marshaled the entire economy for armament, but had no idea it had anything to do with war.

This may seem like a fantastic exaggeration, but this is what you would actually be obliged to conclude if you were to acquit these defendants.

They do protest too much. They deny knowing what was common knowledge. They deny knowing plans and programs that were as public as [Hitler's autobiography] *Mein Kampf* and the Party program. They deny even knowing the contents of documents they received and acted upon. . . .

The defendants have been unanimous, when pressed, in shifting the blame on other men, sometimes on one and sometimes on another. But the names they have repeatedly picked are Hitler, Himmler, Heydrich, Goebbels, and Bormann. All of these are dead or missing. No matter how hard we have pressed the defendants on the stand, they have never pointed the finger at a living man as guilty. It is a temptation to ponder the wondrous workings of a fate which has left only the guilty dead and only the innocent alive. It is almost too remarkable.

The chief villain on whom blame is placed—some of the defendants vie with each other in producing appropriate epithets—is Hitler. He is the man at whom nearly every defendant has pointed an accusing finger.

I shall not dissent from this consensus, nor do I deny that all these dead and missing men shared the guilt. In crimes so reprehensible that degrees of guilt have lost their significance they may have played the most evil parts. But their guilt cannot exculpate the defendants. Hitler did not carry all responsibility to the grave with him. All the guilt is not wrapped in Himmler's shroud. It was these dead men whom these living chose to be their partners in this great conspiratorial brotherhood, and the crimes that they did together they must pay for one by one. . . .

If you were to say of these men that they are not guilty, it would be as true to say that there has been no war, there are no slain, there has been no crime.

A Step Forward for International Law

Benjamin B. Ferencz

Adolf Hitler did not prosecute an aggressive war by himself. He also did not do it with only the twenty-two men who were defendants at Nuremberg. So why single out this handful of Germans for punishment? In fact, many more were tried, but these twenty-two were specifically chosen because of their key roles in the war effort. As this excerpt from prosecutor Benjamin B. Ferencz indicates, however, punishing the individuals was not really the point of the trial. The prosecutors, including the author, were more interested in creating a record for history and for attempting to establish a legal code for international behavior that might serve as an incentive for maintaining peace in the future. Ferencz's comments are from a conference on Nuremberg held over forty years after the trial.

I would like to describe what Nuremberg meant to us at the time, what it has meant in the interim, and, as I look back upon it, what its significance is today. My involvement began before the war. One of the things I did to work my way through law school was to do research for one of my professors who was writing a book on war crimes. As soon as I got out of the Harvard Law School, I enlisted as a private in the artillery, and fought in all the campaigns in Europe. As we began to invade Germany and France, I was sent to General Patton's headquarters to help set up a war crimes division. Soon, my assignment was to go into the

Reprinted from "A Prosecutor's Perspective," by Benjamin B. Ferencz, a paper delivered at the conference "Nuremberg Forty Years Later: The Struggle Against Injustice in Our Time," McGill University Faculty of Law, November 1987, by permission of the author.

concentration camps as they were being liberated, in order to try to capture the criminals or collect evidence for subsequent trials. This experience has had an impact on everything that I have done since then.

When the war was over and the Nuremberg trials began, I was recruited to go back as a civilian with the Department of the Army and help in the war crimes prosecutions. I became the chief prosecutor of the largest murder trial in history. It was the trial of the *Einsatzgruppen*—we could not translate their name—the special extermination squads that had murdered over one million people. They were 2,000 men who, for about two years, did nothing else but march their victims out into the woods and machine gun them and drop them into a ditch, with the help of the local militia, the Latvians, the Lithuanians, the Ukrainians and the local police. We captured their daily reports. We picked twenty-two defendants out of the 2,000 or so who were engaged in those mass murders and put them on trial.

The *Einsatzgruppen* case was one of the so-called subsequent trials. Nuremberg did not consist only of the International Military Tribunal; there were a dozen trials at Nuremberg subsequent to that, at which we tried the next echelon of German government—the SS, the generals and industrialists, the doctors and lawyers—and other leaders.

The Motive for Trials

What were we trying to do? Was it a matter simply of punishing the guilty? In that case, to pick out twenty-two would have been rather absurd. We had something more in mind. First, of course, we wanted to establish a historical record. I should say that the very question of whether we should have trials was a major issue. At one time, the British, noted for their fair play, decided that instead of trials it would be better to just take the German leaders out and shoot them. The Russians, of course, would have gone along with that very eagerly, because they never did quite understand why we needed trials. At one time, even Roosevelt had agreed to that.

But subsequently, under the influence of some very

good lawyers, the United States was persuaded to take the position—which finally came to be accepted by all the powers—that we should have trials. If you decide to shoot people, the question becomes, Whom are you going to shoot, and when do you stop shooting? It was decided that we would give the accused, as Justice Robert Jackson, the chief American prosecutor, said, "the kind of trial which they, in the days of their pomp and power, never gave to any man." And we did. The courtroom was open to the world. Every word that was said in that courtroom was open to the world. Every word that was said in that court-

Law, Not Vengeance

The participants in the Nuremberg Trials were not immune to criticism and chief prosecutor Robert H. Jackson was disturbed enough by the arguments to issue a rebuttal before the trial ended. The focus of his argument was on the charge that the Allies were exacting vengeance on the Germans. In this excerpt from an article he wrote, Jackson makes the point that holding even an imperfect trial was better than judging the defendants summarily and executing them by executive order.

Whatever defects may be charged to the Nuremberg trial, its danger as precedent and its offensiveness to American ideas of justice, liberty and law are as nothing compared to the dangers from killing or punishing people for political crimes by executive order. That it can be "better" or less offensive to notions of justice to kill men without a trial rather than with a trial is a proposition hardly defensible to my mind.

The consequence of giving the top Nazis a genuine trial is, of course, labor, inconvenience and expense. We have had to listen to their excuses, and let the world hear them as well, which at times has been provoking. But it does seem to me that it was the decent and orderly way to proceed and it has produced worthwhile by-products as well.

If we had stood these twenty-two defendants against the wall and shot them "by executive determination," in ten

room was recorded in German and English, and everyone could watch.

My instructions were, and my practice was, to give every single piece of evidence that I had to the defense counsel—and the defense counsel outnumbered us twenty to one—so that they could prepare for trial. It was the fairest possible trial. Some have raised the question about trying persons for crimes that were legislated ex post facto, and some have also noted that this was the first time that there was a trial by the victors over the vanquished. These are fair questions. But if you study the development and evolution

---

years the United States would be defenseless against the suspicion that we did not give them a trial because we could not prove their guilt or because they could prove their innocence. Our position would be as weak as that of the Nazis regarding the Roehm purge, in which, by executive order, they killed without trial and on charges of political crimes many of their opponents. Whatever cause they may have had, they did not submit to any public inquiry and they cannot today escape the inference of mere murder. Such a procedure on our part would lay the foundations for martyrdom and a resurgence of nazism in Germany.

Whatever we ultimately do with these men we will do after an open hearing and upon evidence recorded for the world's scrutiny. We as well as the Nazis can be judged on this record, and we do not shrink from the judgment. . . .

So I think the great lesson which Nuremberg has taught the world, irrespective of the outcome of this trial, is that while a hearing to make sure you are punishing the right men and for the right reasons does take time, does cost money and does allow them to reiterate their defenses, it is worth while. Undiscriminating vengeance and killings without hearings are made obsolete by Nuremberg and only the obsolete minded will mourn the loss.

Robert H. Jackson, "Justice Jackson Weighs Nuremberg's Lessons," *New York Times Magazine*, June 16, 1946.

of the law of war crimes, you will see that it was not the first time that these issues had been faced. These issues were faced after World War I, and at that time the same debate took place: Will there be an international trial, and who will try the accused? After World War I, it was decided not to try the German head of state because aggression had not yet been declared a crime and he had not yet been warned that he might be put on trial for that offense. But, the Germans were warned, the next time around it would be different. There were also a number of warnings given in the course of the earliest days of World War II, when the heads of state of all the Axis powers were told that they would be brought to justice. So it was not quite as ex post facto as it would seem to someone unfamiliar with the history or the evolution of the problem.

The question remains: Why a trial by the Allies? It is regrettable that there was no real choice. It would have been preferable had there been an international tribunal of persons who were completely neutral. But it was very difficult in those days to find anybody who was completely neutral, and politically it was quite impossible. So we did the best we could. It was imperfect, but in many ways it was quite remarkable because these great powers "stayed the hand of vengeance," in Justice Jackson's words, and put their enemies on trial despite the enormity of the crimes that had been committed. That is perhaps the most important thing that came out of Nuremberg: the recognition that your enemy, no matter what his crimes, is entitled to as fair a trial as you can give him.

New Crimes

But we wanted something more than that. We felt that the time had come "for the law to take a step forward," in the words of Justice Jackson, who represented the United States. It was declared in the Nuremberg Charter of the International Military Tribunal—which was drawn up by the four victorious powers speaking, in fact, for the so-called civilized world—that there would be a punishable offense known as the "crime against peace." In the future, anyone who started a war of aggression would be guilty of a crime. Why should one murder be considered a crime and one million murders be considered something other than a crime? So, the law took a step forward and declared that aggressive war was a punishable crime.

Another step forward was the concept of "crimes against humanity." The concept of "war crimes" was an old, well-established one under customary law. But the concept of crimes against humanity was something new. In the past it had been the practice, when acts of genocide were committed against minorities, that only diplomatic intervention was permissible. Governments could send a note of protest saying, "You know, we have heard that Armenians are being slaughtered in your country. We would deplore that action should it be true." That was the limited nature of the permissible intervention by the international community. At Nuremberg, we said that that time was past.

When crimes reach such a magnitude that they offend all of humankind, they are crimes not merely against the state but against humanity. And every nation has a right to intervene and insist that those who are responsible, those who have committed these crimes and their accomplices, be held accountable in a court of law. That was another great step forward that we thought we were taking at Nuremberg. We were beginning a process, a legal process, of moving toward a more humane and rational order. That, at least, was our aspiration and our dream at the time. As a young fellow assigned to prosecute this biggest murder trial in history (it was, incidentally, my first case), I was confronted with the problem of what penalty to ask for. One million people had been murdered in cold blood; there was clear documentary evidence and no dispute about the facts. I had dug many bodies out of mass graves with my own hands. What punishment should I ask for? How could I balance one million deaths against twenty defendants—should I ask that they be chopped up in pieces? You can never really balance the punishment and a crime of such magnitude. I wanted the trial to take law and humanity a step forward.

My opening statement was made on September 29, 1947. In the opening paragraph, I said, "We ask this court to affirm by international penal actions man's right"—by that I meant women as well—"to live in peace and dignity regardless of his race or creed. The case we present is a plea of humanity to law." I think that that reflects what we were trying to do. It was a plea of humanity to allow all people, regardless of their race or creed, to live in peace and dignity. That is what Nuremberg was all about. It was the planting of a seed of what we hoped would be an evolutionary process for a more humane and just society.

Establishing a Great Moral Principle

Thomas L. Karsten and James H. Mathias

Once the Allies decided the Germans should be tried rather than summarily judged, it became important to them to demonstrate that their trials, unlike those of the Nazis, assigned some rights to the accused. By scrupulously applying rules of evidence and creating a panel of judges determined to decide the defendants' fate on the basis of what was presented in open court, the Allies left open the possibility that some Nazis would go free, despite the overwhelming sense of their guilt. Thomas L. Karsten and James H. Mathias, two former members of the American prosecution team, believe this was one of the virtues of the trial. More importantly, these prosecutors attest that the outcome of the trial set important legal precedents that may deter future wars of aggression.

The judgment and verdict in the greatest murder trial in history have at last been handed down. Whether we are satisfied with the acquittal of three and the imprisonment of seven, all of whom were intimately associated with a murderous regime, depends in large measure on whether we view the trial as a political expedient or as a judicial proceeding. If it was intended that the court be the instrumentality for enforcing the political decision of the four great powers that the accused be punished, the court might have taken the position that knowledge of the plan to wage aggressive war should be imputed to persons intimately asso-

From "The Judgment at Nuremberg," by Thomas L. Karsten and James H. Mathias, *The New Republic*, October 21, 1946. Copyright © 1946 The New Republic, Inc. Reprinted with permission of *The New Republic*.

ciated with the Nazi regime, and similarly that association
with such a regime was enough to taint the defendants with
guilt. If this was the purpose of the trial, all of the defendants should have been convicted of the crimes with which
they were charged and sentenced to death. Instead, the court
by its decision has clearly indicated that it conducted a judicial proceeding to determine whether the defendants and
the organizations alleged to be criminal were guilty as
charged on the evidence presented.

Critics of the Trial

There are those who will say that these are but judicial trap-
pings to conceal a political decision and that the acquittals
are the necessary window-dressing. Having participated in
the prosecution, we can unequivocally state that this view
does not square with the facts. In the preparation of the case,
most of us were seriously concerned that the evidence
against Schacht, von Papen and Fritzsche might prove in-
sufficient. As the trial proceeded, it became apparent from
the attitude of the court that to convict any of the accused,
we as prosecutors would have to marshal evidence so pre-
ponderant as to leave no reasonable doubt in the minds of
the judges that the defendants were guilty of the specific
crimes with which they were charged. This is not to say that
members of the prosecution staff do not disagree with some
aspects of the judgment. Mr. Justice Jackson has already expressed his dissatisfaction with the acquittal of Schacht and
von Papen. But dissatisfaction with a court's interpretation
of the evidence is as commonplace as judicial decision.

Is the trial *ex-post-facto,* as charged by some, and for this
reason vengeance rather than justice? Those who say that no
law prohibited the acts of the defendants when committed
overlook the nature of international law. The law of nations
derives from treaty and custom rather than from the acts of
legislatures, and only rarely from decisions of courts. In the
years following 1919 there developed the rule that a war of
aggression was illegal. This rule or custom was evidenced,
among other things, by the Kellogg-Briand Pact outlawing

war, to which Germany was the first signatory. All that remained for this court to do was to punish the individuals who violated the rule.

Under the charter establishing it, the tribunal was authorized to try these defendants for participating in a common plan to wage aggressive war and for the commission of war crimes and crimes against humanity arising from the common plan. Viewed judicially, the court was thus powerless to condemn a defendant merely because he was high in the Nazi hierarchy or merely because he was by our standards an evil man.

Establishing Judicial Principles

We may quarrel with the limitations imposed upon the court, but we must judge the verdict in the light of these limitations. So judged, what has been accomplished? First and foremost, a great moral principle has been judicially established—the principle that the planning and waging of aggressive war is the greatest crime known to mankind and that those guilty of perpetrating it shall be punished. Hardly less important than the principle itself is the recognition implicit in its establishment that national sovereignty is no longer a shield behind which aggressors may take refuge.

Does the establishment of this moral principle mean that no nation will ever again engage a war of aggression? Obviously not. But at the same time we must not underestimate the inhibiting force of such a principle. If we as individuals do not rape, murder and rob, it is not alone because there are laws which prohibit such conduct but because the inherent immorality of the acts has become as strong an inhibiting factor as the fear of punishment. Similarly on an international level, if there are to be inhibiting factors in the conduct of the leaders of nations it must be in part because the community of mankind has declared certain conduct contrary to the conscience of mankind.

We doubt that inhibiting factors engendered by this enunciation of moral principle can be adequate safeguard against the lawless use of atomic warfare. The principle must be im-

plemented by the nations of the world acting in concert under the aegis of a strong international organization having
adequate power to deal with potential aggressors. Unless
this is done the advances made at Nuremberg will be illusory and mankind may again stand on the brink of self-
destruction.

The Hangman of Nuremberg

Jon Marcus

> Though the inclination of many Allied officials after the war
> was to execute all the prominent Nazis, the decision to hold a
> fair trial posed the risk that some of the defendants might be
> found not guilty. Of the twenty-two defendants, an even
> dozen were convicted on all charges and sentenced to death.
> Of those, two escaped the penalty: Hermann Göring commit-
> ted suicide and Martin Bormann was never caught. The
> method chosen for those to be executed was hanging, which
> meant there had to be a hangman. No one was forced to carry
> out the sentences; instead, a call went out for volunteers.
> Joseph Malta stepped forward. Associated Press writer Jon
> Marcus interviewed Malta fifty years afterward and found he
> had no regrets.

One at a time, they dropped through the trap door of the
hangman's scaffold and fell still.

Gestapo boss Ernst Kaltenbrunner. Hans Frank, governor-
general of occupied Poland. Slave-labor czar Fritz Sauckel.
Austrian Nazi Arthur Seyss-Inquart.

In all, 10 of the men who led the Third Reich were
hanged in Nuremberg on October 16, 1946, for crimes
against humanity.

"It was a pleasure doing it," said 78-year-old Joseph
Malta, the U.S. Army military policeman who pulled the
lever. "I'd do it all over again."

Reprinted from "Nuremberg Hangman: No Regrets," by Jon Marcus, an Associated Press
wire story published at www.washingtonpost.com/10/15/96. Used by permission of The
Associated Press.

Malta hanged 60 Nazi government and military leaders but became known as Hangman 10 for executing 10 top Nazis on that one night in the gymnasium of Nuremberg's Landsberg Prison.

"These were the ones that gave the orders," he said. "They weren't sorry for anything."

Malta was a 28-year-old MP when the Army asked for volunteers to hang the men condemned by the International Military Tribunal. He stepped forward, he said, because he had learned during his short time in occupied Germany about the Nazis and their newly exposed crimes.

"Being there and talking to the people there, it was easy for me to decide to do it," said Malta, who had sanded floors in civilian life. "It had to be done."

Malta soon found himself in Nuremberg and face to face with Hermann Goering, the Allies' prize catch.

"He was still the boss then," Malta said. "He told us we wasted too much time. I told him we had to do things by the book. He said, 'When the time comes to get me, I'll be dead.'"

Goering kept his promise, cheating Malta's noose by taking poison two hours before he was to have been executed.

As for the others, they were escorted one by one before dawn to two portable scaffolds Malta had designed so that the trap doors wouldn't swing back and strike the condemned in the head. Stacked nearby were 11 empty wooden coffins, one for Goering and one each for the 10 other condemned men.

A dozen somber journalists and generals from the major Allied powers—the United States, the Soviet Union, Britain and France—looked on as black cloth hoods were placed over the prisoners' heads. A German priest recited a short prayer. Malta pulled the level when he reached "Amen," then went beneath the scaffold with a U.S. Army doctor to cut down the corpse.

Beside Kaltenbrunner, Frank, Sauckel and Seyss-Inquart, Malta executed Hitler's foreign minister, Joachim von Ribbentrop; chief military adviser, Field Marshal General Wilhelm Keitel; interior minister, Wilhelm Frick; General

Alfred Jodl; and anti-Jewish propagandists Alfred Rosenberg and Julius Streicher.

The hangings took just one hour and 15 minutes.

Malta left the Army in 1947 and returned to his civilian job. He keeps a tiny replica of the Landsberg Prison scaffold in the apartment he shares with his wife in this community near Boston.

Chapter 5

Reporting on the Trial

Chapter Preface

A mericans have always had a fascination with the law. Today, courtroom dramas are on television, news broadcasts regularly cover significant trials and ones involving celebrities, and a whole cable network is devoted to the courts. In the days before television, the coverage certainly did not have the same intensity, but the media still covered trials of famous villains like Al Capone and those involving important issues such as the Scopes Trial, in which a teacher was charged with violating a state law against teaching evolution.

Watching the television dramas, it is easy to get the wrong impression of what most trials are like. Real-life attorneys usually are not that exciting and do not get to pound on tables and badger witnesses into confessions. All of the evidence cannot be presented during the interrogation of a couple of witnesses and the case closed in less than an hour. Instead, most trials are dull. They involve months of preparation and the collection and analysis of reams of documents and the questioning of sometimes hundreds of witnesses.

The Nuremberg Trial has also been dramatized for television and the movies, and the story makes for compelling viewing. The real trial, however, was not nearly as exciting. There were dramatic confrontations on occasion, particularly between Justice Robert H. Jackson and Hermann Göring, but most of the trial was far more pedestrian. It consisted of months of discussing documents and examining and cross-examining witnesses about the details of the German bureaucracy, the military command, and the institutions responsible for the Holocaust. The introduction of footage from the concentration camps was one unforgettable moment, but it was particularly powerful because similar evidence was not shown repeatedly.

Television did not yet exist, so the reporters covering the trial for radio and print outlets had to convey a sense of drama even when none existed. Most of the day-to-day activities were too dry and unnewsworthy to merit much attention. As some of the journalists covering the trial relate in this chapter, the trial participants were largely bored, especially by the end, and it was difficult for the reporters to find much to say unless they augmented their basic description of the trial events with interviews and other features about the characters and the atmosphere of the trial. Still, when it was over, it was clear to most people that they had witnessed the trial of the century.

Broadcasting the Trial on Radio

Harold Burson

World War II was brought home to most Americans by journalists writing in major newspapers and magazines and radio correspondents, many of whom would later become the first stars of television news. Today, complaints are sometimes heard about the brevity of news stories; a typical report on the evening news will be only a minute or two. Harold Burson was given fifteen minutes a night just to report on the trial for the military's American Forces Network, but he quickly realized how boring it would become when the day to day events and testimony became repetitious. Burson ultimately incorporated interviews to liven up the broadcasts of the daily events. In this excerpt of an interview with Burson, he describes what life was like for correspondents covering the trial and his impressions of the city of Nuremberg, the lawyers, and the defendants. After the war, Burson went on to found one of the world's largest public relations firms, Burson-Marsteller.

I was in Paris for about four months, through the summer of 1945, into the fall. The early part of November, the commanding officer of the American Forces Network (AFN), a man named Colonel John Hayes, who later became ambassador to Switzerland during the Johnson administration, called me to his office.

He said, "There's a special assignment that is very sensitive that I'd like for you to undertake." I said, "What is

Excerpted from an interview of Harold Burson, in *Witnesses to Nuremberg: An Oral History of American Participants at the War Crimes Trials*, by Bruce M. Stave and Michele Palmer with Leslie Frank. Copyright © 1998 by Twayne Publishers. Reprinted by permission of The Gale Group.

that?" He said, "I'd like for you to go to Nuremberg and cover the trial. We want to give this as much time as it needs, so what we thought we would do is we would start out giving you 15 minutes at nine o'clock." It seemed to me that 15 minutes was a lot of time, but he insisted on starting that way. And he said, "This thing is of such importance that the general who heads up the Information and Education Section of the army would like to meet you. He wants to talk to the person who is going to cover the trial."

It was General Paul Thompson, who later became a senior officer at *Reader's Digest.* He has now passed away. General Thompson gave me what his feelings were. He said, "We've got two missions that we want fulfilled." He said, "The first is we want the troops to know what went on in Germany, and how the Nazis [conducted] the war. The second thing is, we have tremendous evidence that the German people are now relying on AFN as their principal source of news." He said even though a relatively small percentage of the people speak or understand English, many of the leaders do. They wanted the German people to get a full dose of straight coverage.

I have a feeling that the reason the general wanted to see me personally, and talk with me, and know what my background was, is that he did not want anyone who was bringing in any ideological baggage of his own to the issue. He just wanted straight reporting. "This is what happened in the courtroom today." He did not want any interpretation. And so that's what I provided.

What I Knew

Did you have a sense, at that time, what the situation had been in Europe, regarding the Holocaust?

My father was very politically sensitive from the standpoint that he did a lot of reading. I grew up in a household that was very much abreast of current affairs. And also because my mother and father had come from England, there was an interest in Europe that you would not expect to find in the average poor household in Memphis, Tennessee. So like many, I knew that there were concentration camps. I am Jewish. Not in my wildest dreams would I have imagined that it was going on on the scale that it was. But even before I went into the army, I was aware that there was persecution. So I was politically aware. . . .

The City

What was your impression of Nuremberg, as a place?

I had been in a number of devastated cities in Germany. I left my unit in the combat engineers in mid-April. We had already reached the Rhine. I had seen Aachen and München-Gladbach and Frankfurt. Nuremberg was one of the two or three most devastated cities in Germany, Cologne being another one that was really on the ground, flattened.

The thing that was hard for me to realize was Nuremberg was still a city of several hundred thousand people. They were living in the rubble, in the basements of houses that had been destroyed. It was a bleak, cold winter, that winter of 1945–1946. You saw very few men. You'd see women with string bags, carrying what looked like three lumps of coal, three or four sticks of firewood, food stuff wrapped in newspaper. It was really a very tragic sight to behold.

Of course, at the courthouse, they had done a fantastic job of building a setting that looked very imposing. They had state-of-the-art technology at that time: simultaneous translation into four languages. It was more like going into a theater than [going] into a courthouse.

We had assigned seats, and I had a front row seat on the balcony, overlooking the courtroom and the boxed area containing those on trial. And so every day until I left in about mid-March, I saw [Hermann] Göring, I saw [Rudolf] Hess, I saw all the defendants.

The Brits Stand Out

What were your impressions of the defendants, the judges, the American prosecutors, and the prosecutors from the other nations?

To start with the judges, the chief judge, Sir Geoffrey

Lawrence, was a character out of Dickens, just exactly what I would have expected from a lord chief justice. He ran that court with an iron hand. Even though he was relatively short and a little stocky, he projected a sense of authority when he walked into that courtroom. You knew who was in charge, and he did it in a very nice, even-handed way. He didn't yell. He wasn't boisterous. He had a very calm voice. I felt by far he was the outstanding person on the bench. [There were] two Americans—Francis Biddle, who was the principal U.S. judge, and then we had an [alternate] judge, named Judge [John J.] Parker from North Carolina. I felt Biddle was a bright, smart man, but very pedantic, although he wasn't meddlesome. He would get off the point with his questions every now and then. The other two—the French and the Russian judges took no active role in the proceedings. They just sat there.

Among the prosecution staff, the British team was the superior team by far. The person I regarded most highly was the number two person on the British prosecution staff, Sir David Maxwell-Fyfe. He had an advantage over the Americans. He knew the European history, and in his cross-examination, he couldn't be flim-flammed. Their number one attorney who didn't stay at the trial very long was Sir Hartley Shawcross, a very erudite British barrister, but he was not nearly as impressive as David Maxwell-Fyfe.

I think the American delegation was somewhat out of its league. They just didn't have the background they really needed when they came into confrontation. I got to know Justice [Robert] Jackson. I always thought he was there because he thought bigger things were ahead for him, politically. I didn't regard him as any kind of legal scholar.

What about his opening statement, which was supposed to be very good?

It was a very good opening statement. Where there were prepared statements, the Americans did well. They even did well in making their case. Where the Americans showed their weakness was whenever they got into cross-examination, because they just weren't immersed in the history, not only of what had happened in Germany at that time, but what led up to the war.

There's a lot of criticism of Jackson's cross-examination of Göring, for instance.

Göring made mincemeat out of him. As long as Justice Jackson was making the case, as long as he had a lot of young lawyers preparing the written case which was, in effect, read, I think he did very well. But when he came head-to-head—Göring was a tough witness; the military people were tough witnesses. . . .

Did you see Tom Dodd in action?

Tom Dodd, I thought, was one of our better people. I guess, you would have to say that he was the number two American lawyer. He presented a major portion of the case. Of the American lawyers prosecuting that first case, I suspect he acquitted himself with greater distinction than any of the other American lawyers.

There was a man named [Robert] Storey from Texas. He was a railroad lawyer, and I can remember the correspondents commenting he had better get back to his railroad practice before he forgets what it's all about. . . .

Broadcasting

What did you do in terms of the AFN broadcast?

AFN did not have a station in Nuremberg. Munich was the closest station that we could get to. As you can appreciate, telephone lines were at a real premium. When I went to Nuremberg, I took an engineer with me. I did not broadcast. I wrote the scripts. I had a reader who read my script because my Southern accent was even more than probably you detect today. I was never a trained radio announcer type. To my great surprise and discomfort, I found out that no preparations had been made to get us from Nuremberg to our Munich transmitter. We needed a telephone line to get us to Munich. There were relatively few telephone lines in service at the time, and a lot of demand for them. I [had] to go back to General Thompson to get the problem solved just hours before our first broadcast.

There was a priority system that the army had for the use of telephone lines and other utilities. It was army military government, and they were running all the utilities. I kept getting from them, "Sorry, soldier, we just don't have any open time to give you for this purpose." I needed about 25 minutes all told, starting at about seven or eight minutes to nine [o'clock]. I called General Thompson, and he immediately got in touch with his counterpart, and they suddenly found a way to give us a line from the Nuremberg courthouse to our transmitter in Munich. We had a broadcast booth in the Nuremberg courthouse. That was not a problem. And nine o'clock at night was a good time for us because the broadcast booth wasn't in use since it was two o'clock in the afternoon in the United States, and that was a dead news hour period. It didn't start getting heated up until the six o'clock broadcast, which was after midnight in Europe. That's when the studio was busy at the courthouse. So I was able to get the land line, and every evening we went on air. The first evening, we weren't sure we were going to make it because we received approval for the line at five or six o'clock in the afternoon. I found out later that evening, through the Army Signal Corps, that there was a message congratulating me from headquarters in Frankfurt, where our headquarters were. That's the first I knew we had gotten through.

Telling It Like It Was

Was there any censorship?

No. I wrote it, and there was no review whatever of my script. . . .

It was amazing for me as a 24-year-old. I literally was in charge. I started writing when the court was over, usually around four-thirty or five o'clock in the afternoon. It took me about an hour and a half to do a 15-minute script. Then I'd have dinner. I'd always go with the announcer, and he would read my script.

The first few days we reported straight what was happening in the courtroom because it was very dramatic. Certainly before the first week was over I recognized that it was not going to be able to sustain 15 minutes every day. It was going to get very, very boring. So we developed a format where we did about a six- or seven-minute report on the trial, and then we dedicated seven or eight minutes to an interview of someone. I tried to get as many military figures as I could, who had to do with the trial. For example, the prison psychiatrist, the prison psychologist, the officer in charge of the guards. I also had the first interview with Justice Jackson. Every now and then I'd bring in a correspondent whose name was well known. So the broadcast was a combination of straight news and a feature interview. I diligently followed what was going on in the courtroom. Radio news reporting back then was very expository and straight. Today, radio and television is interpretive. We did none of that.

Did you know how the programs were going over, either from those who were higher up, or from GIs or from Germans?

The most immediate reactions I got were from the other news people covering Nuremberg. Other than the BBC, the AFN was the only radio reporting they would tune in to. My report was the only American reportage they heard. They couldn't hear the major U.S. networks. At breakfast in the morning, a correspondent would say, "You know, you had a nice angle there," and, "Tell me how to get in touch with the psychiatrist. I think I'd like to do something with him." . . .

Was there a lot of anti-American feeling at the time?

No, none whatsoever because the Americans were their source [of] anything tangible: extra food, blankets, soap, cigarettes. There was very little in their own economy—not only in Nuremberg, but all over Germany. At that time, the Germans felt very subservient. They were really a defeated people. And again, it was a 70, 75 percent female society. The men, even after the war was over, were kept in [POW] camps for months. You just didn't see very many men in Germany. . . .

When you departed, what were your feelings about leaving?

Well, I was of two minds. My going-in impression was,

"This is mankind's opportunity to establish a rule of law that can be universal, and can serve as a deterrent against genocide, against people committing aggression and planning aggression, a deterrent against crimes against humanity."

As time went on, and by the time I left, I thought that Stalin and Churchill had the right idea. About the only thing that they ever agreed on was that they ought to have a quick court-martial for the defendants and then take them out and shoot them. This became very apparent when the defense started. I got to know a couple of the defense lawyers, and they were at such a handicap in representing their clients. They depended on the prosecution for every document that they needed. They did not have the staffs to back them up that the prosecution had. So here it was, the might of four nations, with all their resources against these 20 lawyers who, I think, were paid by the Allied Commission. But we didn't give them any real resources, we didn't give them any real places to work, and they had nothing themselves, no commercial facilities.

I think justice was done, but I don't think it should have taken the better part of a year—10 months—to arrive at the decisions they arrived at. Telford Taylor's book analyzed the deliberations that were going on behind the scenes, which I was not aware of at the time. There were a lot of trade-offs. It got very political. [The correspondents] were always speculating who was going to get the death penalty and who deserved to get it, and who [was] not going to get it. I guess the one that surprised me in getting [off] totally free was [Dr. Hjalmer] Schacht.

I think he tried to present himself as not being part of the cabal, that he brought expertise, which they used, but he never embraced what they did. But the fact was that he really provided the financing that enabled Hitler to carry out his atrocities. I don't believe Hans Fritzsche should ever have been there. He was there because [Paul Joseph] Goebbels had killed himself. . . .

When you came home, how much consciousness was there of the Nuremberg Trials? Were people tuned into it?

Did they have an interest that you had been there? . . .

There was interest, most of my friends knew there was a Nuremberg Trial, for the first 15 years, maybe. My business associates were in awe that I covered the Nuremberg Trial. So in the circle I moved in, it was a credential. But in the big scheme of things, I think it was just a little blip that happened. . . .

What has been your impression of fictional or historical accounts of Nuremberg, compared to your actual experience?

I think from a standpoint of physical context, they got it right. *Judgment at Nuremberg,* particularly, portrays a bit of pageantry in that courtroom. Well, there was. Right in back of where I sat was a visitors' gallery, and there were visitors from all over who were coming there every day, and they would find this scene awesome, to hear these people—they could almost touch them—who committed, perpetrated all these vile acts. So I think it probably served a purpose in exposing the guilt of the German hierarchy and the willingness of so many Germans that followed them. But I think it was short-lived, and now you've got people denying the Holocaust ever even took place.

But I think it's a story that has to be continually told. People don't like to remember unpleasant things, particularly about themselves. We, in America, have a feeling that the only revolution that was ever justified was the [American] one in 1776. And they totally forget what we did to the Indians. Would I have wanted to miss [the Nuremberg] experience? Absolutely not.

The Anti-Climactic Trial Climax

Rebecca West

> The trial was long and few journalists spent all their time covering the event. Many came and went. One of these was the *New Yorker*'s Rebecca West. In this article, West describes what it was like to return to Nuremberg to hear the verdicts read. She also talks a little about what it was like to be a Jew covering the trial of those who had tried to murder her people, and what it was like for a woman in what she calls a "man's world."

It was the last two days of the Nuremberg trial that I went abroad to see. Those men who had wanted to kill me and my kind and who had nearly had their wish were to be told whether I and my kind were to kill them and why. Quite an occasion. But for most of the time my mind was distracted from it by bright, sharp, smaller things. Consider the marvels of air travel. It was necessary, and really necessary, that a large number of important persons, including the heads of the armed and civil services, should go to Nuremberg and hear the reading of the judgment, because in no other conceivable way could they gather what the trial had been about. Long, long ago, the minds of all busy people who did not happen to be lawyers had lost touch with the proceedings. The daily reports inevitably concentrated on the sensational moments when the defendants sassed authority back. . . .

Excerpted from "The Birch Leaves Falling," by Rebecca West, *The New Yorker*, October 26, 1946. Reprinted by permission of Sterling Lord Literistic as agent for the author.

The Certainty of Death

How much easier would we journalists have found our task at Nuremberg if only the universe had been less fluid, if anything had been absolute, even so simple a thing as the sight we had gone to see—the end of the trial. And we saw it. With observation whetted by practice and our sense of the historic importance of the occasion, we let nothing that happened in the court go by us. We formed opinions about it with edges sharp as honed razors. We knew, when the judges issued a decree that the defendants were not to be photographed while they were being sentenced, that it was a silly and sentimental interference with the rights of the press. Yet about that our opinions were perhaps not so definite as appeared in the talk of the bar. The correspondents who had been at Nuremberg a long time were not so sure about this decree as those who had come for just these last two days. The correspondents who had been in Germany a long time did not appear to like to talk about it very much. It seemed that when one has never seen a man, one does not find anything offensive about the idea of photographing him while he is being sentenced to death, but that if one has seen him often, the idea becomes unattractive. It is not exactly pity that takes one. One would not alter the sentence of death. The future must be protected. The ovens where the innocent were baked alive must remain cold forever; the willing stokers, so oddly numerous, it appears, must be discouraged from lighting them again. But when one sees a man day after day, the knowledge of his approaching death becomes, in the real sense of the word, wonderful. . . .

It was like that in other parts of Nuremberg, where the lawyers lived who had seen every session of the court. They had all been waiting for this day when the judgment would be delivered and the defendants sentenced, for it meant that they would turn their backs on the moldy aftermath of murder and get back to the business of living. But now that this day had come, they were not enjoying it. . . .

There came the day of judgment and the day of the sentences, and I was again aware that I was in a man's world.

Life in Nuremberg was difficult in any case, because of transport. The city is so devastated that the buildings used by the authorities are a vast distance apart, and one cannot walk. Cars are old and rapidly falling to pieces, and the drivers have been out there too long and care about nothing except going home. But when the great day came, there was added a new exasperation in the extreme congestion of the Palace of Justice. It was obviously possible that some Nazi sympathizers would try to get into the court and assassinate the counsel and the judges, and it was obvious

No Escape from the Truth

Today, Holocaust deniers claim that either the Jews were not annihilated or that the atrocities committed against them are vastly exaggerated. As outrageous as their claims are, they still find some people naive or ill-informed enough to believe them. Many survivors of the Holocaust are still alive to bear witness to what really happened, but soon they will be all gone and the only proof of the Nazi horrors will be their recorded testimony and the documentary records uncovered in the Nuremberg Trial and in subsequent trials and scholarly investigation. As this excerpt notes, the Germans themselves, as well as others, might have claimed the stories of their crimes were Allied inventions had it not been for the paper trail established by the Nuremberg Trial. Trevor-Roper was the British intelligence officer in charge of the investigation into the truth of Hitler's death.

W hat will history say of these trials? They are unique, for although special courts have been set up before and political crimes judged by extraordinary authority and although members of defeated governments have been legally prosecuted, no such court has been so universally recognized or its prestige so successfully maintained. The high court that condemned Charles I was never recognized—it was a transitory usurpation. The Riom trials at which the French politicians were tried in 1940 petered out ingloriously. But the Nuremberg tribunal was recognized that the authorities would have to take special care in scrutinizing the passes of the correspondents and the visitors. I had seen myself having to stop at the entrance of the court and show my pass, whereupon a trained scrutineer would examine it under a strong light. Nothing so simple happened. Authority jammed the corridors with a solid mass of military policemen, who again and again demanded passes and peered at them in a half light. These confused male children would have been quite incapable of detecting a forged pass if they had been able to see it, but in this deep

---

even by the defendants, down to the death sentence which it imposed upon twelve of them. . . .

In dealing with the general charges, though the prosecution opened with a sweeping attack, the tribunal at the close delivered a limited judgment. If a man has committed mass murder it is, after all, a secondary matter that he conspired to do it; and it is notable that the heaviest sentence fell on those guilty of the third and fourth charges—of crimes against humanity and war crimes—which are unmistakable in their definition. . . .

Had it not been for this exposure it would have been possible for a new German movement, in ten years' time to maintain that the worst of Nazi crimes were Allied propaganda easily invented in the hour of such total victory. That is now impossible. The most damning documents—the minutes of Hitler's meetings, Ohlendorf's account of the mass murder of 90,000 Jews, Eichmann's account of Himmler's dissatisfaction at a mere 6,000,000 executions, Himmler's grotesque addresses to his SS leaders, Keitel's criminal orders and shocking marginalia—these and many others have now been through the test of cross-examination; their signatures and authenticity have been confirmed. And the real nature of nazism has been confirmed, not by the fallible testimony of report, but by the exacting scrutiny of a court of law.

H.R. Trevor-Roper, "The Lasting Effects of the Nuremberg Trial," *New York Times Magazine,* October 20, 1946.

shadow it was difficult to read print, much less inspect a watermark. This congestion of pass-demanding military policemen occurred at every point where it was necessary for correspondents to move freely, to look around and find their seats, to get in touch with their colleagues. At the actual entrance to the gallery, there was posted a new official, to whom I took a savage dislike because he infringed on a feminine patent. Although he was male and a colonel, he had the drooping bosom and careworn expression of a nursing mother, and he stared at my quite obviously valid pass minute after minute with the moonish look of a woman trying to memorize the pattern of a baby's bootee. Was I irritable? Yes. I and all England, all Europe, are irritable because we are controlled by and sick of organization. And perhaps he was slow and awkward because all people in organization not of the scheming and tyrannic sort are sick of exercising control on resentful subjects.

What did we see in the courtroom? Everybody knows by now. It is no longer worth telling: it was not worth telling if you knew too little; it could not be told if you knew too much. The door at the back of the dock shut on the last of the prisoners, who had worked their final confusion by showing a heroism to which they had no moral right, who had proved that it is not true that the bully is always a coward and that not even in that respect is life simple.

Then the court rose, rose up into the air, rose as if it were going to fly out of the window. People hurried along the corridors into each other's offices, saying goodbye—goodbye to each other, goodbye to the trial, goodbye to the feeling that was like fall. That was if they were the great, of course, for only the great could get out of Nuremberg. The lesser would have to wait at the airport or the railway stations for days as the fog took a hand in the congestion and the planes could not leave the ground safely in the mornings, and more and more people tried to go home by train. On the floor of every office there were packing cases: the typewriters had to go home, the stationery had to go home, the files had to go home. The greater bent down to say goodbye to the lesser, on their knees beside the packing cases; the lesser beamed up at the greater. It was a party; it was like going off for a cruise, only instead of leaving home you were going home; it was grand, it was happy, it was as positively good as things seem only in childhood, when nobody doubts that it is good when the school term comes to an end. Yet if one could not leave Nuremberg, this gaiety did not last intact after the sun went down. Then one heard words that brought back what one felt about the end of the trial, when one did not turn one's mind away from it. A man said, "Damn it all. I have looked at those men for ten months. I know them as I know the furniture in my room. Oh, damn it all. . . ."

Familiarity Breeds Sympathy

That vague, visceral mournfulness, that sympathy felt for the doomed flesh as for the frosted flower, settled on the mind steadily during the days that passed after the return from Nuremberg, as the executions drew nearer. It was dispersed suddenly by the news of [Hermann] Göring's suicide. A dozen emotions surprised me by their strength. The enormous clown, the sexual quiddity with the smile that was perhaps too wooden for mockery and perhaps not, had kicked the tray out of the hands of the servant who was carrying it; the glasses had flown into the air and splintered, the wine of humiliation we had intended him to drink had spilled on the floor. It was disconcerting to realize that the man's world in which Nuremberg had had its being had in effect been just as crazy as it had looked. All to no purpose had the military police fallen over my feet and had I fallen over theirs, all to no purpose had the colonel with the bosom brooded pendulously over my pass. The cyanide had freely flowed. I felt fear. Whether this romantic gesture would revive Nazism depended on the degree to which the people in the waterlogged Europe I had seen from the plane were preoccupied with the spoiled harvest and their lack of shoes. If their preoccupation was slight or desperate, they might equally play with the idea of restoring the Nazi regime. I remembered the incidental obscenities of Nuremberg, such as the slight smell that hung round the door of the room that housed the atrocity exhibits—the shrunken head of the Polish prisoner, the soap made from concentration-camp corpses, and the like; I remembered the vigor of some of the defendants, and the passivity of the German people in the streets, blank paper on which anything could be written. But also there came a vague, visceral cheerfulness, applause for the flesh that had not accepted its doom but had changed it to something else that made a last proof of its strength, such as one might have felt for a beast that has been caught in a trap and that, when its captors come, arches its back and makes a last stand. All the people I had seen fleeing from Nuremberg, who would be halfway across the world now, trying to forget the place, would be straightening up from whatever they had been doing and saying with a laugh, before they could check themselves, "Oh, that one! We always knew he would get the better of us yet."

Chronology

1945

February: President Franklin Roosevelt, Prime Minister Winston Churchill, and Premier Joseph Stalin meet in Yalta and agree to prosecute Axis leaders for war crimes at the conclusion of World War II.

April 30: Adolf Hitler commits suicide in his Berlin bunker.

May 2: President Harry Truman appoints Associate Supreme Court justice Robert H. Jackson as chief U.S. counsel for the prosecution of Nazi war criminals.

May 6: Reichsmarschall Hermann Göring surrenders to the Allies.

May 7: General Alfred Jodl agrees to Germany's unconditional surrender, ending World War II in Europe.

May 23: British troops capture Flensburg, Germany, and capture several top Nazi officials who later would be tried at Nuremberg; Hitler's top aide, Heinrich Himmler, commits suicide.

June 26: Jackson and his counterparts from Britain, France, and the Soviet Union meet in London to decide how to proceed with the prosecution of the Germans responsible for the war.

July 7: While the Soviets advocate holding the war crimes trial in the area they control in Berlin, Jackson proposes the city of Nuremberg; although almost the entire city was destroyed during the war, the Palace of Justice survived and is ultimately accepted as the site for the trial.

August 8: The Allies reach a final agreement on the prosecution of war criminals that is known by the location in which it is signed—that is, the London Agreement.

September 5: Truman decides to name former attorney general Francis Biddle as the American judge at Nuremberg.

October 14: British representative Sir Geoffrey Lawrence is elected president of the International Military Tribunal.

October 19: Indictments are issued against the major war figures.

October 25: One of the prisoners awaiting trial, Robert Ley, former chief of the German Labor Front, commits suicide.

November 20: The trial of the major war criminals by the International Military Tribunal begins at 10:00 A.M. in Nuremberg, Germany.

November 21: The defendants plead "not guilty," and the trial begins with Jackson's opening statement for the prosecution.

November 29: The prosecution shows a film in the courtroom of Nazi atrocities that provides graphic images to supplement the often dry documentary and oral evidence.

December 13: The prosecution introduces particularly gruesome examples of concentration camp atrocities, including examples of human skin with unusual tattoos that were used by the Buchenwald commandant's wife in lamp shades and the head of an executed Pole used as a paperweight by Commandant Karl Koch.

December 18: The prosecution begins its case against the seven German organizations: the Nazi Party leadership, the German high command, the SS, the SA, the SD, the Reich cabinet, and the Gestapo.

1946
January 8: The prosecution begins its case against the individual defendants.

March 6: The prosecution rests its case.

March 8: The defense begins its case.

July 30: The defense of the seven indicted Nazi organizations begins.

August 30: Testimony is completed in the Major War Criminals Trial.

August 31: The defendants are permitted to make statements.

September 2: The justices retire to deliberate.

October 1: The verdicts are announced, and eleven of the twenty-one defendants are sentenced to death.

October 13: The appeals of the convicted Nazis are rejected.

October 15: Göring commits suicide by swallowing a smuggled cyanide pill.

October 16: The ten surviving defendants sentenced to death are hanged in Nuremberg.

For Further Research

Books

Michael Berenbaum, *The World Must Know: The History of the Holocaust as Told in the United States Holocaust Memorial Museum*. Boston: Little, Brown, 1993.

Joseph Borkin, *The Crime and Punishment of I.G. Farben*. New York: Free, 1978.

William J. Bosch, *Judgment on Nuremberg*. Chapel Hill: University of North Carolina Press, 1970.

Central Commission for Investigation of German Crimes in Poland, *German Crimes in Poland*. New York: Howard Fertig, 1982.

Robert Conot, *Justice at Nuremberg*. New York: Carroll & Graf, 1984.

Belinda Cooper, *War Crimes: The Legacy of Nuremberg*. New York: TV Books, 1999.

Jack Fishman, *Long Knives and Short Memories*. New York: Richardson & Steirman, 1987.

Israel Gutman, ed., *Encyclopedia of the Holocaust*. Vols. 1–4. New York: Macmillan, 1995.

Whitney Harris, *Tyranny on Trial*. Dallas: Southern Methodist University Press, 1954.

Joe Heydecker, *The Nuremberg Trial: A History of Nazi Germany as Revealed Through the Testimony at Nuremberg*. Westport, CT: Greenwood, 1975.

Robert H. Jackson, *The Nuremberg Case*. New York: Knopf, 1947.

Michael R. Marrus, *The Nuremberg War Crimes Trial of 1945–46: A Documentary History*. New York: Bedford Books, 1997.

Werner Maser, *Nuremberg: A Nation on Trial*. New York: Scribner, 1979.

Nazi Conspiracy and Aggression. Vol. 4. Washington, DC: Government Printing Office, 1946.

Airey Neave, *On Trial at Nuremberg*. Boston: Little, Brown, 1979.

The Nuremberg Case as Presented by Robert H. Jackson. New York: Knopf, 1947.

Joseph Persico, *Nuremberg: Infamy on Trial*. New York: Viking, 1994.

Drexel Sprecher, *Inside the Nuremberg Trial: A Prosecutor's Comprehensive Account*. Lanham, MD: University Press of America, 1999.

Bruce M. Stave and Michele Palmer, *Witnesses to Nuremberg*. New York: Twayne, 1998.

Telford Taylor, *The Anatomy of the Nuremberg Trials*. New York: Little, Brown, 1993.

Trial of the Major War Criminals Before the International Military Tribunal. Nuremberg: IMT, 1947.

Trials of War Criminals. Washington, DC: Government Printing Office, 1950.

Ann Tusa and John Tusa, *The Nuremberg Trial*. New York: McGraw-Hill, 1985.

Websites

The Avalon Project (www.yale.edu/lawweb/avalon/imt/imt.htm). Part of the Yale Law School online records. The Avalon Project contains many documents on law throughout the world and throughout the centuries. This specific page presents the transcripts of the Nuremberg Trials.

The Nizkor Project (www.nizkor.org). From the Hebrew term for "we will remember," Nizkor is an organization dedicated to preserving the truths about the Holocaust. Its website offers catalogued information on major figures, organizations, and events relating to the Nazi efforts to enact the Final Solution.

Index